Caviar!
Caviar! Caviar!

Caviar service at the Peninsula Hotel, Hong Kong. *Photo: CLIC Studios Ltd.*

Caviar! Caviar! Caviar!

by GERALD M. STEIN
with Donald Bain

LYLE STUART INC.   SECAUCUS, N.J.

LYLE STUART INC.
120 Enterprise Ave., Secaucus, N.J. 07094
Published by LYLE STUART INC.
Published simultaneously in Canada
by Musson Book Company
A division of General Publishing Co. Limited
Don Mills, Ontario

LIBRARY OF CONGRESS CATALOGING IN PUBLICATION DATA

Stein, Gerald M.
    Caviar! Caviar! Caviar!
    1. Caviar.   I. Bain, Donald, 1935-   II. Title.
TX385.S73   641.3′92   81-9235
ISBN 0-8184-0315-2   AACR2

Manufactured in the United States of America
by Kingsport Press, Kingsport, Tenn.

Designed by A. Christopher Simon

TO MY FATHER,
a caviar nut,
who was even more nuts
about Us.

Acknowledgments

In writing any book, an author receives assistance from many people, and it is not always possible to thank each of them appropriately.

Among those to whom I am indebted for their contributions to this book are Marlies Jung and Lonny Kalfus, whose photographs have provided much of the book's beauty; my daughter Elisabeth, who edited the book, took some of the photographs, and prepared some of the recipes and whose ideas and suggestions have been invaluable.

For the elegant design of the book my thanks go to Chris Simon, who worked closely with Arthur Smith and Paul Busby to produce order out of chaos.

A special note of appreciation goes to my wife, Diane, for her inspiration and encouragement. It may be a cliché, but it is nevertheless true that the book could never have been written without her.

G.M.S.

Contents

Caviar!
Caviar! Caviar!

Caviar service on Lufthansa German Airlines. *Photo courtesy Lufthansa German Airlines.*

Foreword

It isn't surprising that I know a lot about caviar. I've spent most of my professional life finding it, judging it, buying it, shipping it, storing it, and selling it. I know caviar the way a cobbler knows shoes, or an astronaut knows outer space.

It's my business—and my love.

I graduated from the Wharton School at the University of Pennsylvania in 1960. It took me four months to realize that I didn't want to spend my life as an accountant. Once that decision was made, I took a job as a warehouseman at Iron Gate Products in New York City. Along with the job came membership in S.O.A.—Sons-in-Law of America. (Yes, I married the boss's daughter!)

Being a warehouseman in a caviar business represented starting on the ground floor in a literal sense. It was my job to clean up after the experienced caviar packers were through packing. It also gave me time to ponder becoming an accountant once again.

I stayed at Iron Gate. I was promoted to packer, then to packing supervisor, then to salesman. Ultimately, I was summoned to the boss's office. "*We* are going to the Caspian," he said.

Since then I've been up to my ears in caviar, in its pleasures and problems, its joys and woes.

That was the beginning of a seemingly endless series of flights to the four corners of the globe in search of a myriad of specialty foods to be served by the finest restaurants to their most discriminating clientele: venison from New Zealand, Scottish salmon, mahi-mahi from Taiwan, Canadian quail, Panamanian shrimp, and of course, Caspian caviar.

Is it a glamorous life?

Of course it is, once the jet lag, customs problems, and lost baggage are forgotten.

I very much enjoy dining in the great restaurants of the world with the people who provide these bastions of gastronomy with the very bread of their existence. Winging to Paris on the Concorde for a dinner meeting with the titans of caviar has a certain panache. Negotiating with the Iranians and Russians, the Panamanians and Taiwanese is not only challenging, but downright exhilarating.

But there's an even greater reward to be realized, and that's the heightened appreciation of the pleasure of fine food on a personal level.

I've come to view dining in a fine restaurant in much the same way an Olympic skier attacks a promising downhill slope. I'm challenged to find the best "course" the restaurant has to offer, and my greatest disappointment comes when the restaurant, *my* downhill slope, fails to live up to the challenge.

The world of fine food is one to which I'm proud to belong.

After almost twenty years as a member of the New York Wine and Food Society, I was elected its president in 1979. This election fulfilled a special place for me in my life, a recognition quite separate and apart from the commercial aspects of gastronomy. It brought into exquisite balance my professional and personal immersion in the world of fine food. I treasure my position of leadership with the New York society as much as the presidency of Iron Gate, which I assumed in 1969.

In this book I've tried to give as broad and deep a view of caviar as possible. I approached every major caviar house in the world, seeking information. My close friends, many of them my competitors, were generous in their help. I thank them for this. We share a close and unique membership in the fraternity of gourmet food.

For those readers who've already tasted and enjoyed fine caviar, I trust this book will offer a complete and interesting look behind the scenes. For those who are still to be initiated into the mystery and pleasures of caviar as a personal and provocative way to please the palate, may I be the first to toast you and your new adventure.

Gerald M. Stein
New York City

ONE

The Mystique of Caviar

MYSTIQUE!

The technological maze through which we muddle these days seems to have stripped away that wonderful thing called *mystique.*

Everything appears to have lost its romantic quality. The legitimacy of pure wool has given way to shiny polyester. Leather is now vinyl that looks like leather—almost.

Numbers have replaced names. Dates with members of the other sex are made through computers. Coats are no longer tossed over puddles to protect the dainty feet of a damsel, and there are footprints on the harvest moon.

Food has suffered the same fate. You can't keep up with the artificial preservatives without a scorecard from the Food and Drug Administration. Too many of the better restaurants serve up "fresh frozen" entrées. And the sacred American hamburger now comes wrapped in yellow paper and is accompanied by a milkshake that tastes like aerated Kaopectate.

Aimé Hatif, the maître d'hôtel at the famed Tour d'Argent in Paris, has been with that restaurant for nearly thirty-five years. He holds the responsibility for selecting and purchasing the caviar for the restaurant. *Photo courtesy La Tour d'Argent.*

THANK GOD THERE IS STILL CAVIAR!

Caviar, little fish eggs extracted from big, burly sturgeon that have spent their lives in the waters of the Caspian Sea, retains to this day that aura of genteel wealth which provides gracious entertaining. Why not? Pound for pound, mouthful for mouthful, caviar is the world's most expensive food. And for those who have been touched by the sinful pleasures of pure beluga malossol plucked from its setting in an elegant, chilled bowl and accompanied to the mouth with chilled Russian vodka or sparkling champagne, it is worth every penny. After all, what price romance?

ROMANCE.

Ah, yes, caviar's place in history is secure as an object of unbridled love. To ply a lovely lady with caviar and dry champagne is to demonstrate to her the good taste and sensitivity only a lover of worldly proportions could possess. Of course, diamonds and pearls work pretty well too, but pound for pound, they are even more expensive than caviar. Besides, when compared to a pound of the best caviar, gems pale as a gift. Any fool knows that a gemstone is precious. Only those who have progressed beyond such clichés and experienced the richness of caviar can truly be counted among gift givers extraordinaire.

The very word *caviar* is part of the public vocabulary. To the world it signifies wealth, good taste, and indulgent living.

Consider the three-act play by Julius Horst entitled *Caviar*. It was set in Saint Germain, near Paris, and in Dijon. The following is from the play.

Two characters, Vanjour and Bouffardin, are speaking. They are close friends.

VANJOUR *(speaking of his wife):* She cooks everything herself. She cooks very well, but ordinary food.

BOUFFARDIN: That is really provincial.

VANJOUR: Yes.

BOUFFARDIN: I suppose mutton chops.

VANJOUR: Our marriage is only mutton chops. I have ruined my stomach. I am a gourmand and choose caviar over mutton. That is why I have had myself called to Nancy on military duty.

BOUFFARDIN: But there you will get mutton too.

VANJOUR: No—there I will have caviar. You see, I am not going to Nancy—but to the Riviera.

BOUFFARDIN: With your wife?

VANJOUR: Wouldn't that be mutton again, you chump! Can't you understand? No, I am going with a charming married woman. A friend of Susan's—she is caviar.

And so it went. The mistress, so revered in French literature, was termed caviar; the wife, poor thing, mutton chop.

This playwright was not the only stage scribe who wrote of caviar. In Act II of *Hamlet,* William Shakespeare wrote, "His play . . . pleased not the million, 'twas caviare to the general." The play he referred to, like caviar, was too good for the masses.

Songwriters, too, have always recognized the instant image conjured up by the word *caviar.*

Rodgers and Hart wrote:

> Caviar for peasants is a joke;
> it's too good for the average man.

Charlie Drew, that pixie of café-society pianists, often sang,

> Caviar comes from virgin sturgeon;
> Virgin sturgeon's one fine fish.
> Virgin sturgeon needs no urgin';
> That's why caviar's my dish.*

As a line in his popular song "All I Want Is You," Cole Porter wrote, "Who wants to tire of caviar? I do."

The mystique of caviar has captured the imagination of the world for generations. There is no other food on earth that allows a hostess to be provident, festive, elegant, and even poetic, all at once. Caviar is the hors d'oeuvre of kings and queens, the favored aphrodisiac of lovers, a source of boundless joy to nobles. Connoisseurs weep over it. Competitors use James Bondian tactics to secure the dwindling world supply. It is flown all over the earth, packed in ice like whole blood being shipped to the battlefield.

*The lyrics of this song are often attributed to an old English toast at caviar feasts:

> Caviar is the roe of a virgin sturgeon,
> And a virgin sturgeon is a very rare fish.
> Very few sturgeons are strictly virgins;
> That's why caviar is a very rare dish.

Caviar service at Maison du Caviar, Paris. *Photo courtesy Maison du Caviar.*

Caviar *is* mystique. Whether it's called *ikra* in the Soviet Union, *Kaviar* in Germany, *khavyah* in Iran, caviar in the United States, or caviare in Shakespearean English, it reigns as the world's most treasured delicacy.

Caviar's history is long. Its mystique and romance remain intact. And because of conditions that will be discussed later in this book, its cost continues to climb. But as J. P. Morgan noted when someone asked him about the cost of maintaining his yacht, "If you have to ask the cost, you can't afford it anyway."

This photograph, taken in 1908, shows a beluga sturgeon weighing about fourteen hundred pounds and containing about two hundred pounds of caviar, which would be worth more than sixty-nine thousand dollars on today's market. The sturgeon was caught at Astrakhan.

TWO

The History of Caviar

Unfortunately for historians of caviar there is no Thomas Alva Edison or Guglielmo Marconi to point to as inventor or discoverer. There is simply no way to ascertain the identity of the first person to open a sturgeon's belly, extract its black, gray, or perhaps even golden eggs, taste them, and exclaim, "Eureka!"

Of course, the probability is that the first caviar taster did not jump for joy over what it did to his taste buds. What makes sturgeon roe into caviar is the addition of just the right amount of salt. Without salt, caviar is just plain old fish eggs.

Where did it begin, this love affair with the black berries?

The early Persians not only liked the fish eggs they found in sturgeon, but attributed a medicinal quality to them. In early Persia, sturgeon roe was known as *chav-jar*, which loosely translated meant "cake of strength." It was prescribed for a whole variety of ailments, including hangovers. To this day, there are those who swear by caviar's therapeutic values, not so much as a cure for a hangover, but for prevention. They may be right—but more about that in the chapter on caviar's nutritional values.

TWA

605 THIRD AVENUE, NEW YORK, NEW YORK, U.S.A. 10016

October 23, 1979

Mr. Gerald Stein
Irongate Products
424 W. 54th Street
New York, N.Y. 10019

Dear Gerry:

It was a tremendous honor for TWA to be selected to carry Pope John Paul II, other members of the Papal Suite, and media representatives from around the world during His Holiness' United States visit and on his return flight to Rome.

All feedback that we have received -- from the Pope and others in the Papal party, guests on the flights, and in media reports -- indicate that food, beverage and inflight service on all segments of the journey were a huge success.

Gerry, we very much appreciate your contribution of the special price for the individual jars of Osetra Caviar served from Washington D.C. to Rome. The inflight crews indicated that the passengers enjoyed both the caviar and the Scottish smoked salmon very much. (After finishing the hors d'oeuvre course, the Pope was too tired to continue eating, so his dinner consisted mostly of Iron Gate products.)

I am enclosing some menus from the Pope's trip that I thought you might like to have as a memento of this historic occasion. Additionally, any pertinent media articles are either included or will be forwarded separately as we receive them. (I assume the New York Post was referring to your product when they listed "Osprey Caviar"!)

Thanks again.

Regards,

Michael T. Duarte
Director - Dining
Service Programs

Enc.

cc: B. Kenyon

TRANS WORLD AIRLINES, INC.

A letter from TWA Dining Service Director Michael T. Duarte, praising the caviar served to Pope John Paul II during his 1979 flights to and from and within the United States. *Courtesy Trans World Airlines, Inc.*

DINNER
Fresh Iranian Osetra Caviar
Prawns   *Pâté de Foie Gras*
Scottish Smoked Salmon   *Celeriac*

CHATEAUBRIAND, SAUCE PERIGUEUX
Château Talbot St. Julien 1970
LAMB RIB ROAST, MINT SAUCE
Moët et Chandon, Brut Imperial
LOBSTER THERMIDOR, RICE PILAF
Freemark Abbey Chardonnay 1977
Rissolé Potatoes   *Tomato Florentine*

Endive, Bibb Lettuce and Tomato,
Vinaigrette Dressing
Sourdough and Pumpernickel Bread
Grissini Breadsticks
Whipped Butter

Brie   *New York Cheddar*
Dunlop   *Gorgonzola*
Gethsemani Cheese from
Gethsemani Farms, Trappist, Kentucky

Assortment of Fresh Fruits

Swiss Toblerone Chocolate Ice Cream
Amaretti Cookies   *French Pastries*
Florida Key Lime Tarts

Trappistine Candies from
Mount Saint Mary's Abbey,
Wrentham, Mass.

Coffee   *Tea*   *Espresso*   *Milk*
Coffee Flavors of the World

CONTINENTAL BREAKFAST
Orange and Tomato Juice
Pineapple Boat
Croissant   *Whipped Butter*
Danish Cheese Pocket   *French Roll*
Damson Plum Jam from
The Trappist Monks of
Saint Joseph's Abbey,
Spencer, Mass.

FEATURE MOVIE
"A Little Romance"
Starring Laurence Olivier
P.G., A-2

SUITE OF HIS HOLINESS
Pope John Paul II

HIS EMINENCE
Agustin Cardinal Casaroli

THEIR EXCELLENCIES
Archbishop Eduardo Martines
Archbishop Jean Jadot
Archbishop John R. Quinn

Bishop Jacque Martin
Bishop Thomas C. Kelly, O.P.
Bishop Paul C. Marcinkus

Monsignor Audrys Backis
Monsignor Virgio Noe
Monsignor Luigi Del Gallo
Monsignor Justin Rigali
Monsignor Taddeuscz Rakoczy

Father Jan Schotte
Father Romeo Panciroli
Father Stanislaw Dziwisz
Father John Magee
Father Roberto Tucci

Reverend Robert N. Lynch

GUESTS
Dr. Renato Buzzonetti
Dr. Mieczyslaw Wislocki
Prof. Valerio Volpini
Sg. Angelo Gugiel
Mr. Steve Falez
Sg. Alberto Goroni
Sg. G. Felici
Sg. Arturo Mari
Maj. R. Buchs
Sgt. P. Hasler
C. Cibin
L. Grassi

A portion of the menu, showing the food (including caviar) served to Pope John Paul II on his TWA flights to, from, and within the United States in 1979. *Courtesy Trans World Airlines, Inc.*

According to Aristotle, the early Greeks, too, enjoyed caviar. No banquet was complete in ancient Greece without heaping platters of the delicacy, carried into the banquet hall by specially selected slaves, heralded by the blare of trumpets. The Greeks even had special flower arrangers to prepare an appropriate setting of garlands and flowers for the black berries.

Caviar appeared on the menu during the classical age of Roman imperialism. So did sows' udders and thrushes' tongues. One of Italy's notable fictional gluttons, Trimalchio, waxed poetic about becoming sated with *caviala*. (Some think that the word *caviala* followed Roman conquest into Turkey, where it became *khavyah*. However, as mentioned, the early Persians used the word *chav-jar*, so the history of our word *caviar* is—perhaps appropriately—lost in mystery.)

Because of its advantages, sturgeon during the Middle Ages was known as the royal fish. When caught, all sturgeon had to be delivered to the local feudal lord.

Pope Julius II was reported to have tasted caviar and liked it. That happened in 1520. More recently, Pope John Paul II enjoyed caviar on the flight between New York and Rome.

As with anything that takes on a magical and almost spiritual quality, caviar has been linked with great events in history. Most of these "reported sightings" are apocryphal. One event, however, stands scrutiny; it concerns a revolution in Russia.

This is what evidently occurred: There was at the time a Cossack leader of Robin Hood proportions named Stenka Razin. Those of the Don country and of the area around Astrakhan probably tend to exaggerate Stenka's feats. He was not the benevolent protector of the little guy as reported. Rather, in today's Mafia context, Stenka was in the protection racket. He and his band of Cossacks extracted payment from Caspian Sea fishermen in exchange for keeping their territory free from Persian and Turkish pirates. There are no reports of Stenka actually having battled the pirates of the Caspian Sea, and speculation is that he paid them off with a percentage of the protection money he'd received from his clients. At the same time

Although Stenka might have had the pirate chieftains in his pocket, his influence did not extend to the higher echelons of Russian government. Like most heads of state, Czar Alexis was trying to balance the budget. One of the schemes he concocted to raise revenue was to impose an excessive tax on salt. This didn't upset those who used salt only as a seasoning, but it was tantamount to disaster to the Caspian fishermen who made their living from the roe of the sturgeon they netted, because without salt there is no caviar.

The fishermen elected a delegation to visit Stenka at his camp. The delegation offered to retain him if he would function as a private army to protect them against the czar. They'd already decided to not pay the tax, and that would mean that the czar's army would be paying them a visit.

Stenka appreciated the confidence the delegation displayed in him but turned its members down. It wasn't that the money wasn't good enough or that the odds weren't right. The problem was that Stenka had recently done battle with the shah of Persia, had won, and had been given, as a gift by the shah, a dazzling young lady who was presently occupying his every waking moment. Maybe he said to the delegation of fishermen, "Stenka is a lover, not a fighter." Maybe he didn't.

At any rate, the delegation returned to the Caspian dejected and pessimistic about the economic future. Until . . . Stenka woke up one morning a few weeks later, looked at the voluptuous creature next to him, looked at his bank book, and made a decision. It was time to be a fighter again. He sent word to the fishermen that he would take up their battle with Czar Alexis.

Stenka's battle plan was this: He would seize a flotilla of barges belonging to the czar, load his band of fearless Cossacks on them, and have them towed up the Volga River to Moscow. There, he assured his clients, he would persuade the czar, either by negotiation or by force, to rescind the salt tax.

The Caspian fishermen lined the banks of the Volga and cheered their hero as he prepared to cast off on his journey. Before he did, however, he couldn't resist a final flash of flamboyance. He stood on the lead barge and sang a song he had composed, "Volga, Volga, Mother Volga."* He completed all ten verses, then gestured for his Persian lovely to join him on deck. When she did, he turned to the crowd and exclaimed, "Stenka is through with love. Stenka now goes to war!" With that, he picked up the Persian lady and tossed her into the river as a sacrifice.

The horses on the banks of the Volga were whipped into motion, and the barges slowly moved upriver toward Moscow.

Stenka's mission to Moscow was not a success. The czar had him arrested, beaten, tortured, and finally quartered. Stenka's band of Cos-

---

*Stenka's authorship of the song remains debatable.

sacks impressed the czar, however, and he kept them on as his personal army. And as we all know, the Cossacks remained as personal body-guards to a succession of czars for more than three hundred years.

The salt tax was never repealed. The sturgeon fishermen raised their prices, and everyone was happy except the consumers of caviar.

Caviar was always considered a delicious treat by those in Russia who had access to it, but it did not achieve its worldwide popularity until it was elevated to the czar's court menu around the turn of the century. And it has always been a favorite, almost a necessity of life, for Russian nobility.

In the late eighteen hundreds, a grand duke of Russia was visiting France. He awoke one morning with an insatiable craving for Russian caviar.

These engravings from *Frank Leslie's Illustrated Newspaper,* August 3, 1878, show sturgeon fishing and caviar production on the Hudson River.

His French host offered him native caviar, but the duke refused. *"Nyet,"* he said. "I must have my beloved *ikra.*"

Two of the grand duke's aides were immediately dispatched to the Paris office of one of Russia's leading caviar exporters. They ordered four hundred pounds of caviar. The agent for the exporter immediately headed for Moscow, where he arrived on a sleigh in the midst of a blizzard. He purchased caviar for twenty-five cents a pound, loaded it in the sleigh, and returned to Paris. By the time the precious black eggs were delivered to the duke, the cost of transportation had boosted the price to more than five dollars a pound. Not that that mattered to the duke. He had enough caviar to last throughout his visit to France, morning, noon, and night. Of course, that kind of craving has kept the price of caviar rising every year since then. Even the substitution of the

MANUFACTURING CAVIARE FROM THE ROE, IN THE CAVIARE CELLAR.

NEW YORK.—AMERICAN INDUSTRIES—STURGEON-FISHING AT HYDE PARK, ON THE HUDSON.—From Sketches by our Special Artist.—See Page 370.

jet airplane for a one-horse open sleigh hasn't helped.

Still, it wasn't that long ago that those with a taste for caviar could satisfy it within a modest budget. Americans enjoyed it as a native dish. Until 1900, this country produced about 150,000 pounds of caviar a year, 100,000 pounds of it from the Delaware River, at Penns Grove, New Jersey. Sturgeon were caught in rivers emptying into the Atlantic and Pacific Oceans. France produced caviar in its Gironde Estuary region. It was also produced in the North Sea, the Baltic, and the Sea of Azov.

In New York, around the turn of the century, a portion of caviar cost what a glass of beer cost—a nickel. American grocers stocked caviar as a staple item. Saloons that offered free lunches laid out caviar alongside Kentucky ham and Cape Cod oysters. In fact, oysters cost twice as much

NEW YORK.—AMERICAN INDUSTRIES—STURGEON-FISHING AT HYDE PARK, ON THE HUDSON—HAULING A STURGEON BY A NOOSE FROM THE NET INTO THE SCOW.—From Sketches by our Special Artist.—See Page 270.

Black gold.

Part of the cold-storage facilities at the Romanoff caviar plant in the free port of Hamburg, Germany, about 1900.

Osetra and sterlet, after a copper engraving by M. E. Bloch (1782).

Silver salmon and hook salmon, after a copper engraving by M. E. Bloch (1782).

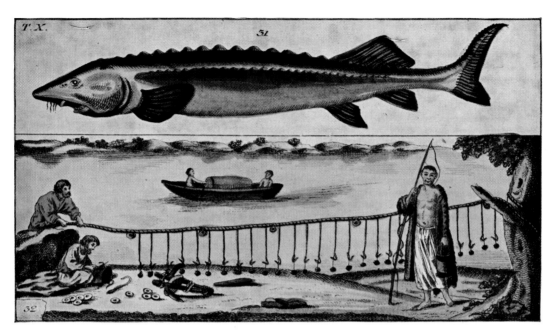

Beluga and hooked snare, from Wilhelm's *Unterhaltungen aus der Naturgeschichte,*
1799.

Sealing and packing tins of caviar at Astrakhan, 1911.

as a serving of caviar in railroad dining cars. You paid no more for caviar on those grand old trains than you did for celery and olives.

The Waldorf and Plaza hotels served it free. So did the Holland House and the Knickerbocker.

But those days are gone forever. American coastal waters became polluted, and the sturgeon gave up. The same thing happened in France.

Today, only Russia and Iran produce quality Caspian Sea caviar. These nations ply the waters of the Caspian in search of the black gold hidden within every female sturgeon's massive belly. And that black gold has played a large part in shaping relations between the Soviet Union and Iran.

Another view of the Romanoff cold-storage facilities.

Net tending on the Volga. *Photo courtesy S.A. Caviar-Volga.*

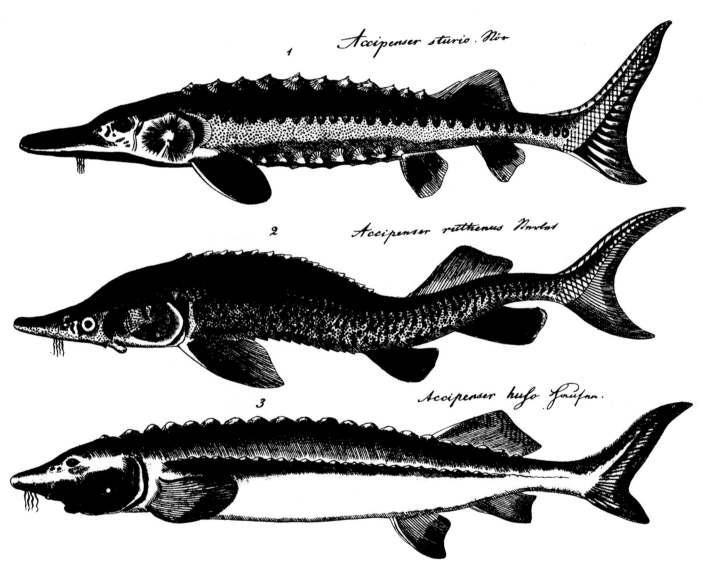

1 Accipenser sturio. Nör

2 Accipenser ruthenus Nordt

3 Accipenser hufo. Haufen.

Drawings of sturgeon. Top: sevruga. Middle: osetra. Bottom: beluga.

T H R E E

A Little About Sturgeon

For those engaged in judging fish beauty contests, it's unlikely that the sturgeon will ever garner the blue ribbon and a featured role in Jaws III.

The sturgeon is a big, lazy fish. It gets its nourishment by lying on the bottom of a sea or river and using its ~~protractile~~, toothless mouth and thick lips to suck up plant life, crayfish, insect larvae, and mollusks. It's like one big, continuously acting ichthyomorphic ~~Electrolux~~. The biggest sturgeon species, the beluga, has such a large and powerful vacuum that it often also takes in carp, bullheads, and herring.

There are three basic types of sturgeon found in the world today, although technically there is a fourth, which has become rare enough to have lost its official category.

The largest species of sturgeon is the *beluga*. This ferocious-appearing but benign-acting monster of the deep can grow to as long as thirty feet and weigh as much as three thousand pounds. But beluga of that magnitude are not the rule. A fully matured female beluga sturgeon usually weighs in at a thousand pounds and runs between fifteen and twenty feet long. If it manages to avoid the caviar fisherman's nets, a beluga will live seventy or eighty years, although a few have been re-corded as having reached the centenarian level.

Because the beluga is the largest sturgeon species, its eggs are the largest too. Roe usually comprises about ten percent of a full-grown sturgeon's weight. If a female sturgeon weighs in, let's say, at two thousand pounds, that means two hundred pounds of sturgeon eggs—caviar. At $250 a pound (as this book goes to press), you can see why netting such a sturgeon is cause for a week of vodka drinking, dancing, and singing in the Caspian Sea fishing villages. Of course, $250 a pound is what the consumer pays. The Caspian fisherman is only the first link in the pricing chain. Still, a big sturgeon catch means plenty of rials or rubles in the family treasury.

The second species of sturgeon is osetra (or ossetrova or ossetrina, depending on your spelling preference; I'll use osetra).

Osetra are the medium-sized sturgeon. They grow to about two hundred or three hundred pounds, and seven feet in length. Because they are a smaller fish, their eggs are smaller. The whole question of which eggs make better caviar will be dealt with in the chapter on caviar types.

The smallest of the three main categories of sturgeon is the *sevruga*. This little lady grows to be about fifty pounds and produces the smallest commercially marketed eggs.

The sevruga has a tender shell and the most aromatic taste of all. A connoisseur of caviar like *Mad* magazine's publisher Bill Gaines, given the choice of beluga, ostera, or sevruga, will always select sevruga.

At one time sevruga was priced at half of what beluga cost. But as caviar fans became savvy, demand for sevruga grew, and now the cost is between two-thirds and three-quarters of the going beluga price.

The fourth species of sturgeon, the sterlet, is now so rare that there is literally almost no sterlet caviar available. This is ironic, because at one time, the most prized fish eggs in the world came from the diminutive sterlet.

Oddly enough, we recently found a single tin of golden sterlet while inspecting a shipment of caviar imported from Iran. I brought it as a gift to René Aponte, former president of the Wine and Food Society of San Juan, Puerto Rico, and owner of one of the largest private wine cellars in the world. Mr. Aponte served the sterlet at a reception at his home, high on a hill overlooking San Juan, to celebrate my fortieth birthday.

The names of various caviars are taken from the types of sturgeon in which they are found. Consequently, there are beluga, ostera, and sevruga caviar.

Beluga caviar, as served at the Wine and Food Society of Puerto Rico.

The author and Malcolm K.
Beyer holding a sturgeon in
the Caspian Sea.

A North American sturgeon.

Iranian beluga sturgeon. *Photo courtesy S.A. Caviar-Volga.*

It takes a long time for a female sturgeon to mature into an egg-carrying mama. Belugas aren't ready to produce eggs until they're eighteen or twenty years old. The medium-sized osetera begin producing in about twelve years. The smaller sevruga start producing eggs in seven to twelve years. This long maturation time, coupled with the devastating effects of worldwide industrial pollution, has dropped to dangerous levels the number of grown female sturgeon carrying a full compliment of roe.

The constantly rising price of caviar is not artificially induced. There is simply a shortage of roe-carrying sturgeon.

In the days when sturgeon were bumping into each other all over the world, caviar prices reflected this glut. At the turn of the century, strollers along New York's Hudson River were used to seeing barges loaded with a couple of hundred large sturgeon on their way to Albany, where the meat was sold for as little as a penny a pound. Sturgeon meat was sold then as "Albany beef."

Sturgeon were so plentiful at one time that they were caught mainly for use as bait to catch more marketable fish. The caviar from sturgeon roe wasn't considered nearly as valuable as was the fish's *balik*, or smoked back. One can only speculate on how many tons of sturgeon roe were dumped as waste.

Interestingly enough, King Henry II of England foresaw a sturgeon shortage. He placed the sturgeon under royal proclamation, like the swan.

One final word about sturgeon and about the techniques used to determine their age: Until recently, even the advanced state of ichthyology had trouble accurately judging a sturgeon's age. With other fish, ichthyologists interpreted the annuli, or growth rings, much as is done with trees. Fish scales carry within them a rather distinct pattern that changes predictably with the aging process.

Sturgeon don't have scales. Their covering is more like armor plate that protects the soft, cartilaginous skeleton. Therefore, sturgeon is not kosher, nor is its roe.

At first, marine biologists determined the age of a sturgeon by analyzing a cross-section of its otoliths, or ear bones. But aging sturgeon lose their hearing. The ear bones crystallize and thus become too difficult to read.

The newer technique is to remove the first bony ray of the sturgeon's pectoral fin, which can be analyzed much more accurately. This is the technique most used today.

Knowing how to gauge a sturgeon's age has little relevance to the caviar lover. It's the roe that counts. But then again, you never know when you will be in a line of people waiting to savor caviar from an elegant serving table. The person directly in front of you might consider himself or herself an unparalleled expert in matters of caviar. Knowing that the sturgeon from which the hostess's caviar was taken had probably gone deaf, depending upon the relative crystallization of its otoliths, you could forever put the expert in her or his place.

Small fish, caught in the sturgeon nets, are shipped to Soviet markets.

FOUR

Choosing Caviar

"Once you've tasted caviar in Europe with borax added, you'll never be content with any other kind."

"Pressed caviar isn't as pretty as whole berries, but it really is superior. Ask any Russian."

"The size of the egg means nothing to me. It's all in the color."

"The color of the egg is irrelevant. It's all in the size."

"It's all the same to me."

And so it goes with caviar. Those who have developed a lifelong taste for it will defend their particular favorite type with all the zeal of a cornered honeybadger. They'll present a list of reasons as long as the Volga, quote every caviar expert who ever lived, and recall with misty eyes the time and place of having swooned over the single best batch of caviar they've ever tasted.

But although each type of caviar does have its own special appeal, it all ultimately boils down to the taste. Savor a good batch of beluga malossol, osetra, or sevruga and the variations in color and egg size become unimportant. A smear of top-quality pressed caviar can make you for-

Some of the various labels that appear on caviar.

get, at least for the moment, the loose, gray eggs of the beluga. The sweeter taste caviar has in Europe, because of borax having been added to it, might well stave off homesickness for the American variety to which only salt has been added—until, of course, you return home and rekindle your love affair with malossol.

However, in choosing caviar for your next party, there are some things to look for.

Trust your nose and follow its lead. Caviar should never smell fishy. It should have a light, oily scent. And if it's even slightly spoiled, it will let your nose know it.

Peculiarly enough, many consumers including self-proclaimed caviar experts still tend to judge caviar by its appearance rather than by its taste.

Mimi Sheraton, food critic for the *New York Times,* came to our warehouse last year to purchase caviar for a New Year's Eve party. She was shown tins of the largest imaginable gray beluga, as well as a light, firm sevruga and some rather soft, dark sevruga. After sampling them, she selected the least eye appealing, the soft, dark sevruga, as the best tasting and bought it for her party.

As is the case with wine, reading the labels on tins of caviar can pay off in increased knowledge and in helping you choose the type and quality of caviar that's right for you.

If the tin contains beluga caviar, it will say so. And if it's lightly salted, it will include the word *malossol.*

If the label says something like "large grain" or "giant grain," the chances are it's osetra.

The country of origin should be on every label. As you now know, nearly all the good caviar comes from either Russia or Iran. If the best is what you're looking for, stick to the product from one of these two nations.

One last word on labels. If it doesn't say *pasteurized,* you can presume it's fresh caviar. Labels seldom bother mentioning that the caviar in the tin is fresh.

Personally, I always look for two things when choosing caviar: light salt and firm grain. For me, caviar perfection means large, firm, gray, lightly salted sturgeon roe.

But the ultimate test is, and will always be, that moment when the visually perfect caviar is placed in one's mouth. Then the taste buds come alive and let you know whether you've just found caviar utopia, sturgeon mediocrity, or "Waiter—bring me shad roe."

   To prove that the best caviar is the one that tastes best, not the one that looks best, I once purposely packed a tin of beautiful large gray but rather salty eggs, to be compared with black but perfect tasting eggs at a tasting held in the duplex apartment of Richard Weissman, a member of the Norton Simon family. Naturally, everyone preferred the good-tasting caviar, and my point was made.

   Before World War II, caviar gourmets found their utopia on the magnificent trans-Atlantic ocean liners. Such floating palaces as the *Bremen,* the *Olympic,* the *Aquitania* and the *Mauretania,* the *Ile de France* and the *Normandie,* the *United States,* and of course, the majestic *Queen Mary* plied the waters between Europe and New York and served the finest great gray berries available. All the caviar served on the ocean liners was preserved with borax. Seafaring caviar contained salt, too, but not as much, since the borax served as a more effective preservative.

This photograph, taken just before a caviar tasting, provides a perfect example of the differences in shade between light and dark beluga caviars.

Salmon roe. *Photo: Marlies Jung.*

Alas, those who still recall those days of beluga on the high seas can no longer indulge themselves in borax-preserved caviar.

It was discovered in the thirties and forties that baby bottles washed in borax were sometimes left with a poisonous film. Therefore, pure-food-and-drug laws now forbid the use of borax in caviar imported to this country, and unless you happen to be on the invitation list to parties at foreign embassies, you'll never taste the sweetness of borax-preserved caviar in the United States.

This country's Food and Drug Administration keeps a close check on caviar that comes into the United States. The borax content is of special concern, and even a trace of that ingredient is cause for an entire shipment of quality caviar to be rejected.

Once, a shipment of Iranian caviar valued at nearly a million dollars was detained by federal inspectors because a minute amount of borax was detected during testing. This can happen for a variety of reasons—a lingering amount of it in a pan or in the screens used to separate the roe from the sack.

Whitefish roe. *Photo: Marlies Jung.*

This particular shipment belonged to Romanoff, and each container had to be individually checked to ensure that no borax entered the American market.

Before moving on to the types of caviar available to the American consumer, one final word about judging the product in a general sense. Any whole-berry caviar should consist of intact, uncrushed berries, each coated with its own fat. Because the fat will tend to rise during shipment, any portion of caviar scooped from the top of a tin might contain some of the fat that should be clinging to berries at the bottom.

As with everything else in life, buying from a caviar supplier of reputation, or from stores with a large turnover, avoids most problems. Those of us in the business of providing the best-quality caviar to our buyers have a certain reverence for it and will settle for nothing less.

FIVE

Varieties of Caviar

I t wasn't long ago in the United States that any fish roe that was black or dark gray could be termed *caviar*. It made no difference how the eggs got to be black or gray, as long as they were. A buyer, thinking he'd purchased a pound of sturgeon caviar, often ended up with whitefish or lumpfish eggs that had been dyed darker than their natural white.

That doesn't happen any more because the law governing the importation of caviar clearly states that only the eggs from sturgeon may legally be called caviar.

That means that if the tin or jar you buy says only "caviar" on it, it's processed from the eggs of the sturgeon. Other types of caviar must identify the source of the eggs (whitefish caviar or lumpfish caviar, for example).

Each batch of beluga caviar receives a numerical designation. There are three such ratings, "0," "00," and "000."

These numbers are representative of gradations in the color of the beluga eggs. The "0" rating is given the darkest eggs, "00" is used for eggs of a medium-dark coloring, and "000" goes to the lightest eggs.

Left to right: 0 beluga, 000 beluga, golden osetra, and sevruga.

Naturally, these ratings are subjective and depend upon the trained eye of the Russian or Iranian expert. However, there is remarkable uniformity in grading. If you pick up a tin of beluga caviar with a "0" rating, you can pretty much count on small black eggs. And a tin with a "000" designation will most certainly contain sturgeon eggs that are pearly gray. But again, color does not guarantee good taste.

Aside from the numerical designations, caviar is classified according to the type of sturgeon from which it comes. (For now, we'll stick to *real* caviar—caviar from sturgeon.)

Beluga caviar comes from the largest sturgeon, the beluga. It is considered by the majority of caviar fanciers to be the finest available today. Because the beluga is the largest fish in the sturgeon family, its eggs are correspondingly large. That simple fact of nature means, for many gourmets, the best caviar. They are willing to pay more for it, and they do. Caviar marked "beluga" commands the highest price on the market.

But let me caution you: Wide latitude exists within every category of caviar. Much depends upon the conditions under which the fish grew and spawned, water temperature and salinity, the water's relative freedom from industrial waste, the age of the fish, and, equally important, the handling the roe received during all phases of processing, packing, shipping, and storage. The large, glistening black berries of the beluga might well represent the best caviar available, provided all the variables went in its favor. But they don't always, and quality within every category of caviar, including beluga, does vary.

If extraordinary caviar is what you want for your next party, keep in mind *malossol*. Malossol is the Russian and Iranian term meaning "little salt." When a particular batch of caviar is judged by the Russian or Iranian experts to be of top quality, they might decide to process it "malossol"—using less than five percent salt in relation to the amount of roe receiving it. In simple terms, one pound of salt is generally used for each *pud* of caviar. A pud is a Russian weight equaling approximately forty-one American pounds.

All types of caviar can receive the malossol treatment. When they do, the cost rises. The reason for this is simple: The less salt used, the more perishable the caviar. The cost of handling, shipping, and storage goes up. The consumer must pay for it.

What all this means is that if you are hosting a party at which you wish to serve the very finest caviar in the world, based upon current standards, you will buy a malossol caviar, probably a beluga. You'll buy it from a reputable dealer who's known for his dedication to the mystique and romance of his product. And you'll serve it with considerable elegance and grace. (The chapter on serving will suggest some ways to enhance the visual appeal of the caviar you serve.)

The next type of caviar you might choose is *osetra.* *(Ossetrina* is the Russian word for sturgeon.) Like beluga, this is named for the type of sturgeon from which it comes. When looking for it you might find it spelled ocetrina, ossetrina, or ossetrova. Don't worry—they all mean the same thing. And the color ranges from brownish to golden.

First-quality osetra caviar tastes every bit as good as a first-quality beluga. It generally has a nutty taste. You mustn't, however, make a taste comparison between a beluga that has been treated as malossol and an osetra that has not.

All things considered, beluga and osetra are equally good unless you simply respond to the visual appeal of larger berries or to the intangible sensual experience of the larger berries in your mouth.

The third type of caviar that you might choose is the *sevruga.* Most caviar served today is sevruga. As with osetra, different spellings are sometimes used. The most common variant spelling is *chivrouga.*

Although the sevruga sturgeon provides the smallest of the three commonly available caviars on today's world market, it is not the smallest in the world. But don't worry about that, because even if your preference is for smaller berries, the smallest sturgeon, the sterlet, is so rare that most of the world's most knowledgeable and devoted caviar lovers have yet to taste its succulent, tiny golden eggs. Rumor has it that in the days of the czars, sterlet roe was quickly wrapped in sable and rushed to the czar's dining table at the palace. It was heralded as "gold caviar," and its worth was equal to that of the precious metal.

The great restaurateur Stuart Levin, formerly of Le Pavillion and now an owner of the Top of the Park Restaurant in New York City, had a special passion for the tiny golden caviar. Obviously, it was a passion that was difficult to fulfill because of the scarcity of the product. Levin had a standing order with Iron Gate that should a tin of the gold berries ever come through our warehouse, he would take it sight unseen and taste untasted.

One day, such a tin did arrive. It wasn't really the "pure gold" variety, but it came close. The berries were tiny and perfectly formed. The hue was golden. I was certain it would please him. I had the tin rushed to Levin's restaurant, where it was placed in a carefully controlled storage area designed for that fine restaurant's caviar supply.

Salmon roe and golden whitefish caviar.

Opened salmon, showing roe (U.S.S.R.).

Later that afternoon, two of Levin's close friends stopped by. I mentioned the delivery of the golden berries, and they became very excited. They would have dinner at Levin's restaurant and enjoy what had been delivered.

Unfortunately for them, Levin wasn't there that night. Try as they might, his friends could not extract from the kitchen the golden caviar.

Why? The chef, one of the finest in the world, had looked at the recently arrived tin of caviar and decided that it contained inferior sturgeon eggs. As far as he was concerned, good caviar was black or gray. Gold caviar was second-rate.

It was probably just as well that it turned out that way, because I'm not sure how Levin would have reacted at seeing his prized golden eggs consumed by others. I assume he had a highly pleasurable personal feast.

Sterlet, or golden caviar, has gone the way of the czars, although some claim that the golden berries are still occasionally harvested and served to members of the Soviet Presidium and, when he was still alive and in power, to the shah of Iran.

So if smaller eggs are your preference, you'll have to be content with sevruga, which, by the way, is excellent. Again, first-quality sevruga is conceptually as good as beluga. It doesn't cost as much and does not have the aura of beluga malossol, but it satisfies the most demanding of palates.

There you have the three main choices in caviar—beluga, osetra, and sevruga. Add the dimension of malossol, and you are serving the world's finest to your guests and to yourself.

But now let's move on to a type of caviar that has little to do with the fish that produced it. It consists primarily of rejected, broken eggs. It has the consistency of a gooey mass of tar or of marmalade. And yet it is the most revered caviar for many gourmets and is the hands-down favorite of most Russians. The Greeks prize it over all other types.

It's pressed or compressed caviar, and it deserves special mention.

The sturgeon eggs that go into pressed caviar are either too small to be included in a batch of whole-grain beluga or osetra, having fallen through the wire mesh over which the roe sack is run during processing, have broken during that same process, or are too ripe to be preserved whole.

These magnificent misfits are gathered together in a cheesecloth sack. This is placed in a machine that compresses the sack and its contents from six sides, much like a cotton baler or grape press. As the compression of the eggs takes place, about a third of the fatty liquid is squeezed from the sack, leaving the gelatinous mass known as *pressed caviar*.

Pressed caviar made from top-quality beluga, osetra, or sevruga is shipped in the same sort of tins used to transport whole-grain caviar. A large quantity of the pressed variety is often packaged and shipped in vacuum-sealed jars.

Certain epicurean delicatessens sell pressed caviar in tubes. You squeeze it out like toothpaste. It can be quite good.

Much of the caviar, whole or pressed, that is sold on supermarket shelves has been pasteurized. This gives it a shelf life that would be impossible with fresh caviar shipped in tins, which must be iced continuously and used quickly. But a word of caution is in order. Unlike many other foods that achieve an almost indefinite shelf life through pasteurization, caviar will not keep forever without damage to its flavor and appearance.

And lest you worry that pasteurization significantly alters caviar's flavor, it does not. Yes, any form of caviar that has been artificially treated to achieve longer keeping power can never taste the same as fresh caviar. But the alteration in taste and consistency is not as great as one would imagine.

In Russia, pressed caviar is called *paiusnaya*. It's also called "magnificent" by Russians in the know about the joy of spreading *paiusnaya* on black bread and sipping chilled vodka along with it.

And in America, connoisseurs, to whom taste matters more than appearance, share the Russians' love of the pressed variety.

Finally, pressed caviar costs about forty percent less than whole-berry caviar. When you consider that it's made from the same eggs as the whole-grain type, its appeal is heightened even more.

If you wish to serve caviar at your next social gathering and want "real" caviar, as it is defined by gourmets and the federal government, you need only buy those types I've mentioned.

But you aren't limited to the three major categories (four if you include pressed caviar). The eggs of any fish roe can be served as a caviar dish, and some of them offer a special visual appeal where certain recipes are involved.

Aside from the popular and legal definition of caviar, literally any fish egg can be served as caviar. With sturgeon becoming increasingly rare (and sturgeon caviar prices reflecting this in staggering increments), there is a growing market for roe from a wide variety of other fish.

Such plebeian fish as pike, carp, flounder, bream, cod, and whitefish are providing caviar of a sort to the public. Some of these eggs are dyed, artificially preserved and flavored, and marketed around the world. Shad, Pacific barracuda, mullet, bluefish, mackerel, and dolphin (the fish, not the mammal) are also donating their roe to the worldwide caviar market. And let's not forget the lumpfish, which seems to have become particularly popular.

Another roe that is extremely popular is salmon roe. The eggs of the salmon are red, and numerous recipes specify the use of red berries. But before we take a closer look at salmon, let's see what you might expect when buying caviar taken from whitefish and lumpfish, the two most popular substitutes for sturgeon.

The whitefish is relatively small. It generally weighs between two and six pounds. Its natural habitat is the Great Lakes. Ironically, this substitute for the vanishing sturgeon school is also dwindling in population. Each year sees the price of a four-ounce jar of whitefish caviar going up.

Beluga caviar, ready to be served at a tasting.

Pressed caviar. *Photo: Marlies Jung.*

000 beluga. *Photo: Marlies Jung.*

Center: beluga caviar. Surrounding it, clockwise beginning at twelve o'clock:
American sturgeon caviar; white fish roe; pasteurized sevruga; pasteurized salmon
roe; osetra caviar; fresh salmon roe; sevruga caviar.

American caviar. *Photo: Marlies Jung.*

Russian osetra caviar. *Photos: Marlies Jung.*

Lumpfish is the other most popular fish from which caviar is obtained. Lumpfish are sluggish and thick-bodied. They're found in northern waters of the United States and are also imported in great quantity from Iceland. Their roe tends to be small and gritty. Unlike whitefish, whose roe is lightly salted, lumpfish berries are usually heavily salted and are not as pleasing to the trained palate as those of the whitefish.

Salmon provides a caviar of special note. Salmon roe is red or dark pink. Unlike other roe, which is sometimes dyed, the natural color of salmon eggs gives them a certain appeal that needs no embellishment or altering.

Incidentally, I know people who place an order with their local fish market for fresh salmon roe. There's really no reason why the roe can't be delivered along with the whole fish. Generally, the roe will be delivered in the salmon's skein, a very fragile membrane that contains the eggs. You'll need a little advice on separating the roe from the skein and on salting it to taste, but it's worth the effort. Salmon roe, while not as delectable as sturgeon roe, has a wonderful taste of its own. And by salting it yourself, you get away with using less salt than is used in preparing a commercial batch for sale in your local supermarket.

Russian sevruga caviar. *Photo: Marlies Jung.*

Russian beluga caviar. *Photos: Marlies Jung.*

FINEST IMPORTED

BELUGA
CAVIAR

PRODUCT OF USSR

NET WT. 2 OZS.

DISTRIBUTED BY IRON GATE PRODUCTS CO., INC., N.Y. 10019

An exterior view of the world-famous Petrossian.

SIX

How Caviar Is Processed

S alt, plus experience and skill, holds the key to turning sturgeon roe into caviar. The entire process takes no longer than fifteen minutes; yet the judgment behind the addition of salt can take a lifetime to acquire.

In Iran and the Soviet Union, the salt blender in a caviar plant holds a social position akin to nobility. He is a national hero, a celebrity, a figure deserving of veneration. It is he (or she) who, after careful scrutiny of the sturgeon eggs that have just been extracted from the fish's belly, makes an instant determination as to exactly how much salt should be added and what type of salt it should be. It is also the salt blender who uses his hands to thoroughly mix the salt and the eggs, a task that demands all the dexterity of a brain surgeon. Sturgeon roe is extremely delicate. Broken eggs do not good caviar make (except in pressed caviar). The blender works his particular art with pride and devotion. He knows that somewhere in the world, a gourmet with an exceptionally refined palate will lift that specific batch of caviar to his mouth, close his eyes, recall all the past caviar he has ever tasted, and exclaim either, "It must be the work of Nikolai Nikolayevich Zhizhin; no one else could have done it," or, "Phooey! It must be the work of an apprentice."

Speaking of Nikolai Nikolayevich Zhizhin, Russia's foremost caviar expert for more than sixty years, it has been reported that he once said, "Of every hundred men who enter caviar making, only five become experts, about twenty just make the grade, while the other seventy-five throw up their hands and give up in despair." TO (3) #

With a few exceptions, caviar processing has changed little over the years. In Russia, jars are now filled by machine instead of by hand and most caviar processing is now performed by women.

Let's go back a bit and pick up where the sturgeon is caught. The process differs slightly between Russia and Iran, but the basic principles are the same. Since I've spent more time in Russian caviar plants, I'll describe it from the Soviet point of view.

The fishermen, Tartar types, proud and vigorous, string nets across the tributaries that feed the Caspian Sea. Their boats are not fiberglass runabouts. They're old wooden hulls powered by ancient engines that always seem about to quit.

The boats pull the nets into circles. Close by, but outside the nets' area, stands a large barge, maybe thirty or forty feet long.

Net tending on the Volga.

Brigadier General Malcolm K. Beyer, dubbed the Caliph of Caviar, helping a central-Asian Russian work the net winches.

The Russians who work the net winches have a Mongolian appearance.

Once or twice a day the fishermen enter the nets in the hope that amid the wide variety of fish trapped in them will be a sturgeon, preferably a female one worth, because of her eggs, at least fifty times more than a male.

When a sturgeon is discovered corralled in the net, the fishermen quickly inspect their captive. At this moment, a sturgeon's lack of beauty is most apparent. Its thick-lipped smile is toothless. Large, watery eyes appear filled with resignation. Four whiskers that appear to be made of rubber dangle aimlessly from its face.

"Female!" a fisherman exclaims. *"Caviar!"*

The sturgeon is stunned by a sharp blow to its head with a wooden club. If it had been a male, as is usually the case, it would have been hit,

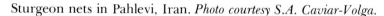

Sturgeon nets in Pahlevi, Iran. *Photo courtesy S.A. Caviar-Volga.*

Removing caviar from sac in Iran. *Photo courtesy S.A. Caviar-Volga.*

then dumped into the barge for later delivery to the fishing stations at Astrakhan.*

But since this is a female, old enough to be carrying eggs, the fishermen *immediately* bring her to Astrakhan, where a trained crew of handlers are waiting.

One of the basic differences between the Iranian handling of a recently caught sturgeon and the Russian method is in how quickly the processing takes place. In Iran, it is some time after the fish has been killed before the roe is removed. In the Soviet Union, the roe is removed before the fish is dead. There is no better way to ensure peak freshness.

The captured monster from the sea is stunned again before being dragged onto a stainless-steel trolley and into the processing room. The room is spotless, worthy of any hospital operating room. Workers wearing white coats and hats stand by to handle the prize catch of the day.

Before the roe is removed, the fish is weighed and its roe is assigned a number. That number will follow that roe to every corner of the world. It's like being given the brand of the cow that supplied your filet mignon.

Once the number is assigned, a woman wielding a scalpel deftly makes a long incision into the sturgeon's belly. With gentle hands, she and others remove the roe sacs and place them on a grating that looks very much like an oversized tennis racket. The openings in the grating are slightly larger than the eggs in the sac. Slowly, with deliberate care, the sacs are manipulated over the grating. Below, a stainless-steel bucket catches the eggs as they are disengaged from their tenuous security in the sac.

Fresh, clear water is added to the buckets. This washing process allows all foreign matter to float to the surface.

Once the eggs are clean, the master salt blender enters the picture. He, too, is dressed in white. His hat is taller. He is the master chef about to sample the award-winning sauce, the taster of the fine wine before it is bottled, the quintessential expert who will decide the fate of the sturgeon's eggs and, by extension, the fate of caviar lovers in France and Japan and the United States.

He makes his determinations. Size of eggs? Color? Will it carry the designation of 0, 00, or 000?

*Astrakhan is the only other city in Russia besides Moscow to have a Kremlin. It was a vacation spot for the royal family.

Caviar being graded in Iran. *Photo courtesy S.A. Caviar-Volga.*

Brigadier General Malcolm K. Beyer (center) grading caviar in the Soviet Union.

The author (second from right) and General Beyer inspecting a Russian caviar plant.

Where is it to be shipped? If France, he will use a borax-and-salt mixture instead of pure salt. There'll be no borax if the shipment is headed for the United States or Germany.

Keep in mind that the higher the salt content, the drier the caviar; therefore, heavily salted caviar loses its firmness quickly.

The decision is made. If the grade is fine enough to become malossol, so it shall be. Only the finest grade of sturgeon roe will be deserving of this treatment. If the eggs are judged worthy of becoming malossol, an amount of salt not exceeding five percent of the net weight of the eggs will be added. Usually, four and a half percent will suffice. TO → 73

But a decision must also be made about the type of salt to be used. Recently, connoisseurs have noticed a delicate difference in the taste of Iranian caviar. This is probably because Iran is now buying salt from the Soviet Union. Grades of salt differ dramatically, particularly in their

The Soviet Union's second Kremlin, at Astrakhan.

Crude as it may seem, this pasteurizing machine produces the finest pasteurized caviar in the world.

General Beyer tastes some caviar prior to shipment.

grind, and Russian salt that is deposited at the mouths of rivers after inundations is considered among the best.

Salt does more than preserve the sturgeon eggs. The heat generated by salt actually cooks the eggs. Raw roe is usually soft and tasteless, and the eggs have no "separateness." The salt takes care of these problems.

Before 1914, salt from the salt seas in the Astrakhan Steppe was almost exclusively used for the preparation of Caspian caviar. This salt contains some chlorine, and to free it from this chlorine, it was stored for seven years in a dry room. The price of fresh sea salt was around five kopeks per pud, but caviar makers were willing to pay a ruble per pud for this stored salt—providing a very good return for the amount of capital invested.

Nowadays, a chemically purified salt is used for the preparation of caviar. As early as 1800 we have proof from reports from Pillau that salt from Lüneburg was also exported to Russia in considerable quantities for the preparation of caviar.

The salt is kept moving in the roe long enough for it to form a pickle with the moisture of the roe. The threads of fat, of which there is a small amount present in the roe, are dissolved and absorbed by the salt.

Then the salted roe comes onto fine hair sieves, which are well shaken until the pickle has run off and the caviar is dry. The tins well known to the trade, with their lithographed prints, their inside lacquer coating, and their sunken lids, which will press into the caviar, must stand ready opened at the preparation of the caviar. The caviar, once the pickle has been sieved off, must be put into the tins as quickly as possible before it "settles," that is, loses its pliability.

So immediately after the salt blender has worked his magic, the caviar is packed into the six-inch-diameter tins. The number of the fish and the grade given the eggs by the blender are affixed to the tin, which is secured with large rubber bands to form an air-tight seal. Now it's ready for the next step—shipping it to points around the globe. With such a delicate product as caviar, transportation demands as much care and skill as does processing. Tolerances are small, variables numerous. Even the most minute mistake can prove costly to everyone involved.

Bad TO =|=

The author (center) and General Beyer with the plant manager and a female caviar blender, determining the amount of salt to use for a particular lot of caviar.

A barrel of caviar being weighed before air shipment from Iran. *Photo courtesy S.A. Caviar-Volga.*

Caviar barrels ready for shipment. *Photo courtesy S.A. Caviar-Volga.*

Caviar packers in Iran, packing caviar prior to air shipment. *Photo courtesy S.A. Caviar-Volga.*

Number-two grade caviar being placed in barrels before shipping. *Photo courtesy S.A. Caviar-Volga.*

Iranian caviar packers. On the floor is woven straw, the material traditionally used to cushion caviar tins for air shipment. *Photo courtesy S.A. Caviar-Volga.*

At a luncheon given for the author and General Beyer at Astrakhan, after a caviar inspection, the meal consisted entirely of caviar, bread, and spirits.

An employee weighs caviar at Petrossian.

Russian osetra. *Photo: Marlies Jung.*

SEVEN

How Caviar Is Shipped

The troubles inherent in shipping caviar do not apply to that which is pasteurized, a practice used more and more these days. The Russians pasteurize caviar in their own country and ship it that way. The Iranians ship the caviar fresh and have it pasteurized at its destination.

The problems arise when caviar is shipped fresh and natural, with only salt to preserve it.

Temperature is critical. If a tin of caviar freezes, it is worthless when it thaws out. It becomes gummy.

If, however, it should be in a temperature above 40 degrees Fahrenheit for a short time, it spoils. Caviar must be maintained within a temperature range of 26.5 degrees to 32 degrees Fahrenheit. Because of its salt content, it does not freeze at these temperatures.

The oil in each black berry within the tin poses its own problem during shipping. Because the fattest portion of the caviar tends to rise during shipment, a concerned shipper will see that the tins are turned frequently to ensure an even distribution of fat. Often, when a large shipment is at stake, the importer will personally accompany it, thermometer in hand, carrying a portable alarm clock to remind him to check the temperature every few hours. Should these precautions not be taken, it could mean that a batch of prime caviar will arrive in less than prime condition, the berries not whole, each individual berry not glistening like a black pearl in its own special fat.

In a word, economic disaster.

And with the shortage of caviar becoming more pronounced each year, no one, especially the consumer, can afford to see a caviar shipment go amiss.

Caviar shipments have sometimes arrived ruined. Once, just before World War II, a shipment from Astrakhan was placed in a ship's refrigerator hold by mistake. It froze. By the time it reached New York it was worthless. The insurance carrier paid off to the tune of more than one hundred thousand dollars. The eggs had been the best of the spring catch, beluga malossol. That was not a good year for American caviar lovers.

In 1966, I was involved with a shipment that ran into problems. At that time the Russians packed their tins of fresh caviar in barrels—fifty-four tins to a barrel, each tin weighing four pounds. The space surrounding the tins was filled with ice from the Volga River.

Before leaving Leningrad, each barrel was weighed. This initial weight was crucial, because if a barrel lost weight at any time during the voyage, it could be safely assumed that some of the ice had melted and that damage had been done to the caviar.

This particular shipment traveled via Stockholm. It remained there overnight before being loaded onto a ship bound for America.

In the morning, the barrels were weighed. There had been a weight loss of approximately twenty percent. Based upon this, our insurance carrier paid an amount equal to the projected loss of revenue from this shipment of caviar. The caviar hadn't spoiled, but its grade would have to be lowered before sale.

I was involved in another problem in which a large shipment from the Soviet Union arrived in less-than-perfect condition. Shipping might have had something to do with it, although it was our conclusion that the original quality of caviar shipped was not up to the terms of the contract.

I worked at the time for Malcolm K. Beyer, a tough, handsome retired Marine Corps brigadier general who was one of the caliphs of the caviar trade and who played a pivotal role in the nationalization of Iran's caviar industry.

General Malcolm K. Beyer holds palate-cleansing hot tea while tasting caviar in the
U.S.S.R.

The author (left) and General Beyer before loading caviar onto an airplane. *Photo courtesy UAS Saarinen.*

I tasted the shipment when it arrived in New York. Beyer would have said, "It has all the flavor of old, recently used sweat socks." (I prefer to describe bad caviar as smelling like dirty diapers.) Either way, bad caviar is obvious to those in the business of judging it.

The problems surrounding this shipment were compounded because it had arrived on December 18. It was counted on to help fulfill the crush of orders that always come in at the holiday season.

Malcolm Beyer cabled Moscow and informed his caviar contacts there that the shipment was unacceptable and that he wished to return it.

Moscow's cable to us was less than encouraging. In fact, it said plainly that the shipment could not be returned.

Beyer, a man of action, picked up the phone and called Moscow. His message was direct, delivered in a booming voice. "Here's what I'll do," he said. "I'll damn well sell your spoiled caviar here and make damn sure the buyer knows it's Russian caviar. And *that,* my friend, will be the end of Russian caviar in the United States."

The Russians saw the logic of Beyer's thinking. He was told that the shipment could be returned provided it arrived in Leningrad by midnight of the 21st. If they had the caviar by then it could still be marketed in West Germany.

It seemed impossible to meet their demands. But General Beyer did not consider anything impossible. Space on an SAS jet cargo plane was immediately booked, and Beyer met the flight in Helsinki.

Loading caviar for air shipment from Finland. *Photo courtesy
UAS Saarinen.*

Caviar is loaded onto a plane in Europe . . .

There was no time for sleep. A seven-ton diesel tractor-trailer truck was waiting at the Helsinki airport to accept the iced load of Russian caviar. Beyer rode up front, next to the Finnish driver. Howling winds blew snow across a road that was partially covered with ice. The driver was good. He maneuvered the big rig expertly over the ice, fishtailing at times, seeming to go hopelessly out of control at others. But he held the road, and the Finnish-Russian border eventually appeared ahead. It was now 11:30 at night, December 20.

The driver stopped the truck and watched with Beyer for a sign that the border would be open to them. At that time of year the border at that point was normally closed, but Moscow had assured Beyer that special arrangements would be made.

Soon, against the black scrim of a star-studded sky, two white flares burst into the darkness, backlighting snow that had begun to fall. The driver put the truck in gear and approached a lonely sentry shack that stood directly on the border. The driver stopped next to the shack and waited. It was ten minutes to midnight.

Five minutes later a pair of red flares from the Russian side were shot into the sky.

"That's it," Beyer barked to the driver. "Let's go."

The truck slowly inched into Soviet territory. Two Russian soldiers appeared from the woods and signaled for the driver to halt. The soldiers jumped up on the truck's runningboards, guns drawn, and motioned for the windows to be lowered.

The soldier on Beyer's side pushed his revolver through the window and asked, "*Gaspodin* Beyer?"

"*Da,*" Beyer replied.

After scrutiny by the soldier that seemed an eternity, the driver was told that he could proceed and that Leningrad would be notified that they were on their way.

General Beyer and the load of Russian caviar arrived in Leningrad at 4:00 A.M. on the 21st. By 10:00 that same morning the shipment had been loaded on another truck and Beyer had been handed his two-hundred-and-fifty-thousand-dollar refund. He slept until late in the afternoon, then caught a flight home and was in his office the following afternoon.

The irony, of course, was that although the general had accompanied the caviar on a reverse trip, he had to nursemaid it as carefully as if it had been on its way to America from Russia.

Fortunately, there was enough caviar on hand in New York to satisfy

. . . and is unloaded in New York.
Photo courtesy Scandia Foto.

holiday consumers in the United States. And presumably, West German caviar lovers had an abundant supply for Christmas.

My own trips to the source of Russian and Iranian caviar have left me with many memories, most of them exciting and rewarding.

My first trip to Leningrad was in the sixties, before there was direct air service between the Soviet Union and the United States. I was there in May. The temperature was 5 degrees Fahrenheit. Inside the refrigerators, the temperature was kept at a constant 28 degrees, the perfect storage temperature for fresh caviar. We kept warm by frequently entering the refrigerators.

On that trip to Leningrad, I first learned how effective tea is to clean the palate between tastes of caviar. The Russian women who worked in the Leningrad caviar facility always had a pot of hot tea going. Undoubtedly, the tea was there more for the warmth it produced than for its palate-cleansing properties. But I discovered that hot, plain tea is an excellent beverage to use when caviar tasting, and I've been using it ever since.

My first trip to Astrakhan occurred in 1965, when I accompanied General Beyer to the north shore of the Caspian Sea and we made our purchase of the spring catch of sturgeon eggs. It was an excellent catch. Like wine, caviar has its good and less-than-good vintages. This particular spring, the fish had been plentiful and large. The roe extracted was generous and of top quality. General Beyer and I were delighted, and we returned to New York heady with the success of the trip and with the pleasure of knowing that our most demanding consumers would be delighted with that season's caviar offering.

"I think we ought to celebrate," the general told me. "Let's have a party with some real caviar lovers."

The list was made up, and the invitations went out. The officers of the leading New York gastronomic societies were invited, including the grand officers of Les Chevaliers du Tastevin.

The great connoisseur Edward Lavin was invited. So was the legendary I. M. ("Tex") Bomba, the importer of Dom Pérignon. Edward Benenson, grand officer of many gastronomic organizations, accepted, as did Paul Spitler, former United States head of the Confrérie de la Chaîne des Rôtisseurs, Clementine Paddleford, then food editor of the *New York Herald Tribune,* Jan Owen, executive secretary of the Wine and Food Society of New York, Charlie Berns, chairman of 21 Brands, Gregory Thomas, head of Comanderi de Bordeaux, a wine-oriented society, and the day's special guest, the Soviet ambassador to the United Nations, His Excellency, Nikolai Fedorenko.

Platters of caviar of every description were served. Ambassador Fedorenko, who was a marvelous linguist, told a number of after-dinner stories that delighted everyone at the table.

This party, to celebrate the spring 1965 caviar catch, was, to quote General Beyer, "One of the better parties that I've ever attended." That was one of the things most of us loved about the general—he wasn't too modest to make such a claim for his own party.

There is considerable waste in caviar. It's tasted upon arrival in New York, prior to being repacked in consumer tins, and that which doesn't make the grade is either downgraded and sold as lesser quality or thrown away. One thing that cuts down on waste is the practice of having the number of the sturgeon from which a batch of eggs was taken

Malossol caviar from the U.S.S.R. *Photo: Marlies Jung.*

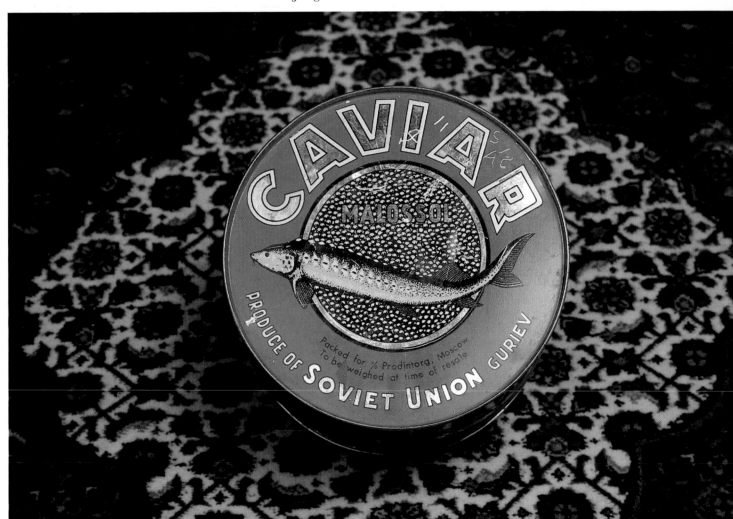

Harrods beluga malossol. *Photo: Marlies Jung.*

accompany every tin. Tasting from one tin then suffices for the entire batch.

I've always been somewhat amused at the visual aspect of a newly arrived batch of precious, top-grade caviar. The tins in which beluga malossol caviar arrive are generally pretty beaten up. The rubber bands that hold the lids on are hardly the sort of device one would expect for a food item bringing more than $250 a pound. Actually, the reason rubber bands are used is to allow for flexibility. Eggs frequently settle during a journey, and to compress them too rigidly would be counterproductive.

There was a time during the heyday of trans-Atlantic steamship travel when theft of caviar was a problem. Workers on the ships would

Iron Gate malossol. *Photo: Marlies Jung.*

sometimes steal a tin or two and sell them to restaurants when they reached port. But this problem has gone the way of the steamships themselves.

One New York physician provides medical treatment for two airline stewardesses in exchange for the tiny tins of caviar they steal from their flights. And members of the diplomatic service often purchase caviar at duty-free prices, bring it through customs in their pouches, and sell it at a profit.

Basically, caviar is valuable but not negotiable. There is a black market in Iran—local fishermen will occasionally attempt to privately mar-

Insulated carriers, used to transport caviar. *Photo: Marlies Jung.*

ket the eggs from a sturgeon catch, but the shah, before his downfall, kept a tight lid on such things.

As you can see, there are basically three steps taken before caviar becomes a delectable reality on your buffet table. The female sturgeon is caught, the eggs are processed, and the caviar is transported to where you can buy it. Of course, it isn't all that cut and dried. It takes a long time for a female sturgeon to mature and develop eggs. But once she does, palates around the world are tickled. As any gourmet can attest, the results are definitely worth the wait!

→ To next page

EIGHT

Storing Caviar

It should be obvious that any food demanding such perfection in shipping would demand equally meticulous handling in storing. It should also be obvious that the ideal thing to do is to eat your caviar as soon after you purchase it as is humanly possible. But that doesn't mean you can't store caviar for a short time.

Pasteurized caviar holds up better than fresh. But even with pasteurized caviar, don't buy any more than you expect to use within a three-month period. It should be stored under the same climatic conditions as fresh caviar, that is, between 26.5 and 32 degrees Fahrenheit.

Sometimes during long storage, pasteurized caviar will develop tiny white specks. These are crystallized protein derivatives and are as harmless as tartrate crystals in wine. They do, however, detract from the caviar's visual beauty.

With fresh caviar, it is best to serve it within one or two weeks of purchase. Fresh caviar should have a heavy, oily aroma. That's good. But let your nose be your guide. If caviar is spoiled, the spoilage can't be disguised from any but the most inefficient of noses.

Should you buy a sealed tin of fresh caviar (repacked by your supplier after he's received it in the original tins with the rubber bands), it will have a shelf life of a few weeks, provided it's refrigerated properly and remains unopened. But once it's opened, throw a party. It simply won't keep. Vacuum-packed caviar, on the other hand, will keep approximately four months.

There are times (not often) when there will be some caviar left over after a party. Assuming it has been chilled in a bowl of ice throughout the party, it can be recapped and used again. If you do this, turn the container over each day to ensure that the oil will reach all the eggs. If you've dipped into a container, take a knife and level off what's left. This will ensure that there aren't any holes into which the oil can run, thus taking it away from some of the berries.

And before recapping, cover it with a layer of waxed paper. Anything you can do to keep the air out will help.

At Iron Gate Products, our caviar-storage rooms are wired into a central alarm system, just as a burglar alarm might be wired. The alarms are hooked up to sensitive thermometers. The moment the temperature goes above or below a predetermined level, the alarm goes off at a central security office in Manhattan. The people in that office immediately call a repairman. Then they call me. It's a little like being a doctor on call. I've been called at 4:00 A.M. I've been summoned out of parties, contacted while traveling, and pulled away from family dinners. Usually, the alarm has gone off because of a malfunction in the system and not because the temperature has changed. But either way, the value of those fish eggs in our storage room is so high that we can't afford to take chances.

So storage of caviar boils down to caring, really. Considering the price of caviar, to not care would be akin to allowing an expensive automobile to rust away.

NINE

Insuring Caviar

Naturally, when you're dealing with a commodity as delicate and perishable as caviar, insurance companies play a significant role in the business.

All caviar companies insure against spoilage during shipment and storage. And we all have our favorite tales about dealing with our insurers. But I don't think any insurance story matches the experience of Arnold Hansen-Sturm when he was at Romanoff.

Romanoff had not made a claim against its insurance company for more than thirty years, even though there were incidents in which insurance might have been paid. It wasn't an oversight on the firm's part, just a management philosophy. Potential claims represented small amounts of caviar—a barrel here, two barrels there. Management felt it would make more sense to save its claim privileges until hit with a truly major loss.

The insurance company that held the policies on Romanoff evidently understood how Romanoff's management was thinking—or at least, its computer did. After thirty years of never having to pay a claim, the insurance company informed Mr. Hansen-Sturm that it was canceling all insurance coverage for Romanoff.

"Why?" Arnold asked.

"Because our computer has predicted that you're due for a major claim within the near future. You've become a bad risk."

Romanoff's caviar is now insured by another company.

TEN

The Iranian-Russian Connection

The commercial history of caviar is very much bound up in intricate and tenuous relations between two countries, Iran and Russia.

These two nations share an interesting body of water, the Caspian Sea, an elongated salt lake that sits between southeastern Europe and Asia. It is the largest inland body of water in the world.

The Caspian's northern arc, which is very long, nudges gently into Russian soil. Its southern shore, which is only about three hundred miles long, borders on northern Iran.

Each spring, female sturgeon point their noses south and head for the warmer waters of the Caspian's southern, Iranian littoral, where they lay their thousands of eggs. Waiting for them are the fishermen who net them, club them, and remove the eggs, which become caviar.

On the surface it would seem that having the sturgeon choose Iran's shoreline for depositing eggs would give Iran an edge in the caviar market. But until recently, this wasn't the way it worked.

In 1893, Iran gave the Russians a franchise to fish, process, and export all its share of the Caspian's caviar catch. That franchise was renewed from time to time, but with each renewal, the inequity became clearer to the Iranians.

In 1953, Malcolm Beyer was brought into the picture with the hope that he could help break the Soviet monopoly system in caviar. Beyer was then president of Iron Gate Products. He was given a leave of absence from Iron Gate in order that he might become naval attaché to Iran. He carried with him his extensive experience in the field of international negotiation, as well as his proven expertise in the world of caviar. He worked closely with Iranian leaders in their efforts to lay the groundwork for what they hoped would eventually become a nationalized Iranian caviar industry. Time was important. The most recent agreement with the Soviets would expire that year.

Under the terms of the agreement that was to end in 1953, Iran received only fifteen percent of the profits realized by the Russians from their processing and marketing of Iranian caviar. Even that small percentage was misleading, because the Iranians were forced to sell their caviar to the Russians at drastically reduced prices. Further, the Iranians were not allowed to inspect the books kept by their Russian partners. A clause in the agreement called for the managing director of the

Robert Delalagade, patriarch of the world caviar industry, has worked at the same desk for more than sixty years.

enterprise to be alternately an Iranian and a Russian, but that clause was ignored. The managing director was always a Russian.

It has been estimated that Russia took from the Iranian shores caviar and sturgeon worth about two and a half million dollars a year during the late forties and early fifties. Iran's yearly cut from this was about a hundred and twenty thousand dollars.

February 1953 approached, and with it the termination of the treaty. Iranian officials were engaged in serious debate over the wisdom of going it alone. Financially, there was no debate. Iran's percentage was absurd.

But those within the Iranian government knowledgeable about caviar processing were concerned that the state of the art had not been sufficiently honed by Iranian processors. It was one thing, they argued, to catch the sturgeon, kill it, and extract the black berries. It was another thing to handle them, salt them, pack them, and ship them. Had the Russians sufficiently educated their Iranian counterparts so that the caviar sold under an Iranian nationalized system would equal that sold by Russian processors?

There was no definite answer to that question. The consensus was that it would have to be assumed that Iranian salters, packers, and shippers were as good as the Russians. Besides, if Iran waited for the Russians to complete the education process for Iranian caviar handlers, the Caspian Sea might dry up in the interim.

That was not out of the realm of possibility. The Caspian had, by that time, dropped almost eight feet in depth because of evaporation. Added to that fact of nature was the danger from increased industrialization of the mighty Volga River, the primary source of fresh water into the Caspian. Sturgeon need plenty of deep, fresh water in which to lay their eggs. From Iran's point of view, their shores were going to become the only place to which the sturgeon would swim. That realization was enough to move the decision in the direction of not renewing the treaty with the Russians.

Besides, nationalizing industry was no longer novel to Iran. It had recently booted out another foreign concessionaire, the Anglo-Iranian Oil Company.

One night in February 1953, Iranian Premier Mohammed Mossadegh summoned Soviet Ambassador Ivan Sadchikov to his office and informed him that the sturgeon treaty would not be renewed.

The Russians took the news hard, although they had cheered when the Anglo-Iranian Oil Company suffered a similar fate.

It had been done. Iran's national caviar industry had become a reality. Malcolm Beyer's role in the decision was rewarded. Iron Gate received Iran's first caviar contract.

But things are never as simple as they seem. The Soviet Union quickly became one of Iran's biggest customers. The Russians do consume considerable caviar; however, most of the Iranian imports are repacked and exported as Russian caviar. Fortunately for the caviar lover, it all adds up to a superior product. Whether he buys Iranian caviar from Iran, Iranian caviar packaged in Russia, or pure Russian caviar, he's assured of getting the finest in the world.

Of course, in the best spirit of competitive international marketing, spokesmen for Iran and the Soviet Union make periodic claims of offering a superior product. The Russians speak of processing skill that has been handed down from generation to generation. They talk of taking the berries from the sturgeon at precisely the right moment in the spawning cycle—too soon, underdeveloped berries; too late, soft berries. The Iranians brag of their own processing skill and sensitivity in choosing just the right moment in the sturgeon's cycle.

Jostling between nations has always played a large part in the caviar story.

In 1939, Robert Delalagade of Caviar Volga in Paris, the world's largest wholesaler of caviar, visited Moscow. He had a complaint. It seems that his only major competitor in Europe, a German exporter, was receiving more caviar from the Russians than was being allocated to his own Paris-based company.

He discussed it with the director of Soviet caviar exports. "We are French and allies," he said. "They are Germans and the enemy. Why so much more to them than to us?"

The director smiled at him. "Mr. Delalagade, we like you, and we have enjoyed doing business with you. But after all, we must take care of our brothers-in-arms."

Delalagade stared at the Russian. Was he telling him something that he wasn't saying?

On returning to Paris, Delalagade went immediately to the office of Premier Daladier to report the conversation.

"It is nothing," he was told. "You are imagining things."

"I am *not* imagining things," he insisted as he was led out.

Three days later, Daladier phoned Delalagade. "We owe you an apology. You were right and we were wrong. The Russians have just announced the signing of a nonaggression pact with Nazi Germany."

CAVIAR TASTING
Thursday, 16 February 1978
Belvedere Suite, Rainbow Room
❖

Fresh Keta and Pasteurized Salmon Roe
❖

Pasteurized Iranian and Russian Sevruga
Fresh Pressed Caviar Iranian
❖

Fresh Sevruga Malossol Caviar Iranian
❖

Fresh Osetra Malossol Caviar Iranian
❖

Canadian and Russian Smoked Sturgeon
❖

Fresh Beluga Malossol Caviar
Russian & Iranian
❖

Perrier-Jouët "Fleur de France" 1973
Stolichnaya Vodka
❖

CHAIRPERSONS: JANET YASEEN, GERALD STEIN

The Wine and Food Society, inc.
NEW YORK

Deladier was surprised, but Delalagade was not. He knew it was coming. A little caviar had told him so. . . .

My favorite story involved the French and Russian ambassadors to the United Nations.

The French ambassador invited the Russian ambassador, Fedorenko, for dinner at the French mission. The culinary staff in the French kitchen went all out to prepare a truly splendid meal for their visitor, who besides being a diplomat of high standing was known to possess great intellect and an appreciation for the finer things of life. A typical Russian dinner was prepared and served—caviar, chicken Kiev, red cabbage, blinis—and Russian vodka and champagne.

After dinner, Fedorenko was asked what he thought of the Russian champagne that had been served.

He thought for a moment, cracked an elfish smile, and said, "I find it as satisfying as French caviar."

Fedorenko's comment caused much laughter among the guests, and it was soon widely quoted at parties and in gastronomic journals.

It all comes back to the same thing, however. Caviar comes from the brackish Caspian, and those who catch the sturgeon and process her eggs do it with skill, dedication, and love. Politics have nothing to do with the ultimate delicacy of gourmets the world over.

Blue Ribbon Caviar Tasting

JULY 15, 1979

Swiss Chalet

THE ONE HUNDRED AND FOUR MEETING

LIMITED ATTENDANCE

FIRST COURSE

Pasteurized Salmon Caviar	Canada
Fresh Salmon Caviar	Canada
Fresh White Fish Caviar	U. S. A.

SECOND COURSE

Fresh Pressed Caviar	Iran
Sturgeon Caviar	U. S. A.
Pasteurized Sevruga Caviar	Russia

THIRD COURSE

Atlantic Smoked Salmon	Canada
Atlantic Smoked Salmon	Scotland

FOURTH COURSE

Sevruga Caviar	Iran

FIFTH COURSE

Beluga Caviar	Iran
Beluga Caviar	Russia

SIXTH COURSE

Lake Sturgeon	Canada
River Sturgeon	U. S. A.
Osetra Sturgeon	Russia

SEVENTH COURSE

Golden Osetra Caviar	Iran

EIGHTH COURSE

Salad and Cheese Souffle	P. R.

NINTH COURSE

Tropical Sherbets	P. R.
Petits Fours	

TENTH COURSE

Cafe Noir	P. R.

WINES

FIRST TO THIRD COURSE — ICED VODKA STOLICHNAYA

FOURTH TO NINTH COURSE — PIPER HIEDSIECK BRUT 1973

COMMENTATOR — Gerald M. Stein

HOSTS — Elsa and René Aponte

MAITRE D'HOTEL — Frank Steiger

بركَ مشخصات وشرايط مزايد خاويار

شركت سهامى شيلات ايران مقدار ٢٧٥ تن انواع خاويار تهيه شده بانمك خالص محصول سالهاى ١٣٥١ ـ ٥٢ ـ ٥٣ ـ ٥٤ ـ ٥٥ ٣ مطابق با ١ مارس ١٩٧٢ الى ٢١ مارس ١٩٧٧ خود را از طريق مزايد هبراى فروش وصدور بكشورهاى آمريكائى وخاورد ورواسترالیا بامشخصات وشرايط زيربفروش ميرساند .

١ ـ مورد معامله انواع خاويار براى مدت پنج سال ودر هرسال ٥٥ تن بانواع وارقام زير خواهد بود :

خاويار دان بلوگا رقم يك	١٠٠٠٠ كيلو
" " " دو	١٠٠٠ "
" " استرا " يك	٤٠٠٠ "
" " " دو	٢٠٠٠ "
" " سوروگا " يك	٩٠٠٠ "
" " " دو	٤٠٠٠ "
" فشرده " يك	٣٠٠٠ "
" " " دو	٢٠٠٠ "
جمــع	٥٥٠٠٠ كيلو

تبصره ـ شركت سهامى شيلات ايران مجاز ومختار است تا ميزان ٢٥ ٪ اضافه يا كمتر از مقدار هريك ازانواع وارقام ٥٥ تن خاويار مزبور در هرسال بخريدار تحويل دهد . دراينصورت اضافه مزبور تابع كليه شرايط درقرارداد خواهد بود .

٢ ـ درصورتيكه شركت سهامى شيلات ايران درنتيجه مقتضيات صيد نتواند ظرف مدت يكسال تمامى انواع وارقام تعهد شد مرا بخريدار تحويل دهد سعى خواهد نمود كمبود آنراد رصورت اقتضاى صيد درسالهاى بعد ازهمان انواع و

Cahier des charges et des conditions d'adjudication du caviar

La Société des pêcheries Iraniennes (Sherkat Sahami Shilat Iran) vend par voie d'adjudication une quantité de 275 tonnes de caviar traité au sel pur produit de son exploitation des années solaires 1351 - 52 - 53 - 54 - 55 correspondant au Mars 21, 1972, jusqu'à Mars 21, 1977 pour la vente et l'exportation aux pays Americains, à l'Australie et à l'Extrème Orient selon les specifications et conditions suivantes

Article 1 - L'objet de la transaction : différentes éspèces de caviar pour une période de 5 ans, à raison de 55 tonnes par an, comme suivant :-

Caviar en grains Beluga sorte No.1	10000 kilos
Caviar en grains Beluga sorte No.2	1000 "
Caviar en grains Oscetra sorte No.1	4000 "
Caviar en grains Oscetra sorte No.2	2000 "
Caviar en grains Sevruga sorte No.1	9000 "
Caviar en grains Sevruga sorte No.2	24000 "
Caviar pressé sorte No.1	3000 "
Caviar pressé sorte No.2	2000 "
Total	55000 "

Remarque - Le vendeur se reserve le droit de majorer ou diminuer jusqu'à 25 % la quantité de 55 tonnes du caviar en proportion des différentes sortes et espèces de caviar qu'il doit livrer par an. Dans ce cas le surplus sera sujet aux conditions spécifiées dans le contrat.

Article 2 - Au cas où, pour des raison dues aux conditions de la pêche, le vendeur serait incapable de livrer la totalité des sortes de caviar qu'il s'était engagé, selon le contrat, de livrer pendant une année, il tâchera de compenser dans les années suivantes et de livrer

Contract for caviar purchase in Persian and French. *Courtesy Iron Gate Products, Inc.*

ELEVEN

The Contracts

Don't count the profits from caviar.
before you catch the sturgeon.

—RUSSIAN PROVERB

The Soviet Union and Iran handle the issuing of caviar contracts in quite different ways.

Since 1952, the Iranians have conducted auctions at which competitive companies bid for the right, usually on a five-year basis, to sell caviar to selected portions of the world. Often, multinational groups band together to make a bid, as do cooperative commercial interests. There's a provocative ring of intrigue inherent in marketing caviar, and the route taken with certain contracts has all the trappings of an elaborate CIA–KGB–Interpol–Scotland Yard–FBI motion-picture scenario.

The Soviet Union generally issues its caviar contracts on a more open-market, fair-trade basis. You might say the Soviets are downright capitalistic when compared with Iran.

Until the fall of the shah, the Western Hemisphere Iranian contract belonged to Panacaviar, headed by George Fixen, a French Swiss who makes his home in Spain. The caviar involved in this contract is marketed through a Panamanian group that uses Puerto Rico as a base. By the time the Iranian fish eggs reach their ultimate destination in the United States, South America, and the Orient, many other nations, cartels, and individuals have been involved.

Mr. Fixen is not a man to be envied these days, with the unrest and political upheaval in Iran. Intrigue is one thing—but where big money is involved and the product is as fragile and as scarce as caviar, what once might have been intrigue can turn into nothing more than one big headache.

The bulk of the European contract is held by a firm known as Caviar Volga. It's owned by that remarkable gentleman Robert Delalagade, now ninety years old, whom I mentioned in an earlier story. Mr. Delalagade insists that caviar is an aphrodisiac and cites his own prowess to prove it. Aphrodisiac or not, Robert Delalagade certainly deserves the unofficial title of the duke or baron of caviar.

He has a magnificent apartment on avenue Foch and a sprawling country estate outside Paris. He works from his world supply headquarters (except to the United States and Russia) at 17 rue Jean Mermoz and crosses the Champs Élysées each day at noon to visit his caviar restaurant, La Maison du Caviar, at 21 rue Quentin Bauchart.

Robert Delalagade has been one of the world's greatest caviar salesmen for more than sixty years. His walls are filled with memorabilia from the early 1900s, when his customers included the great restaurants and hotels of the western world.

In 1924, Delalagade sold seventy tons of caviar. This year he will sell fifty tons. He estimates that in the years between 1924 and 1979 he has sold thirty-five hundred tons of caviar. That's ninety-eight million ounces of the black pearls, figured at fourteen ounces to the caviar pound.

Of course, things have changed since Mr. Delalagade started selling caviar. At the turn of the century, he sold his caviar for about $3 a pound. Today, that same pound goes for more than $250, and the price increases constantly.

The European contract for caviar with Iran, currently held by Caviar Volga, is a yearly one, and is auctioned off through madame Devallou, who always maintained close ties with the shah of Iran. Incredibly, madame Devallou remains the power behind the European caviar contract, despite the shah's fall.

For the purpose of sale, and export of different sorts of Caviar, products of the Iranian Fisheries Company, to American countries, Australia and the Far East, this agreement is drawn up between Sherkat Sahami Shilat Iran (the Iranian Fisheries Company) hereinafter referred to as (Seller), on one part, and _____ hereinafter referred to as (Buyer) on the other part. The Buyer confirms that it is with complete knowledge of the transaction's specifications and his own engagements, that he signs this agreement.

Clause 1 - The Seller undertakes to deliver to the Buyer, for a period of 5 years from 1st of Farvardin 1351 corresponding to 21st March, 1972 a quantity of 275 tons of caviar on the basis of 55 tons per year, of all sorts of caviar treated with pure salt the product of years 1351 - 52 - 53 - 54 - 55 (21st March 1972 to 21st March 1977) under conditions inserted in this agreement and as per following specifications:

Beluga caviar	- 1st quality 10000 Kgs at	U.S. $	per kilo
" "	- 2nd quality 1000 Kgs at	U.S. $	per kilo
Oscetra "	- 1st quality 4000 Kgs at	U.S. $	per kilo
" "	- 2nd quality 2000 Kgs at	U.S. $	per kilo
Sevruga "	- 1st quality 9000 Kgs at	U.S. $	per kilo
" "	- 2nd quality 24000 kgs at	U.S $	per kilo
Pressed "	- 1st quality 3000 Kgs at	U.S $	per kilo
" "	- 2nd quality 2000 Kgs at	U.S $	per kilo
Total	55000 Kgs		

نمونه قرارداد فروش خاویار

بمنظور فروش وصدور انواع خاویار محصول شرکت سهامی شیلات ایران بکشورهای آمریکائی وخاور دور واسترالیا بین شرکت سهامی شیلات ایران که دراین قــــــرارداد (فروشنده)و کــه (خریدار) نامید همیشود قرارداد زیر منعقد میگردد و خریدار اقرار مینماید که با اطلاع کامل از مشخصات معامله وتعهدات خود این قرارداد را امضاء میکند .

ماده ۱ = فروشنده متعهد مینماید که درمدت پنج سال از تاریخ اول فروردین ماه ۱۳۵۱ مطابق ۲۱ مارس ۱۹۷۲ مقدار ۲۷۵ تن از قرار هرسال پنجاه و پنج تن انواع خاویار های تهیه شده بانمک خالص محصول سالهای ۱۳۵۱-۵۲ ۵۳-۵۴-۵۵ خود را بشرح زیر وباشرایط مندرج دراین قرارداد تحویل خریدار نماید .

خاویار دان بلوگا هر قمیک ۱۰۰۰۰ کیلو از قرار هر کیلو دلار امریکا			
" "	دو	۱۰۰۰ " "	" "
استرا "	یک	۴۰۰۰ " "	" "
" "	دو	۲۰۰۰ " "	" "
سوروگا "	یک	۹۰۰۰ " "	" "
" "	دو	۲۴۰۰۰ " "	" "
فشرده "	یک	۳۰۰۰ " "	" "
" "	دو	۲۰۰۰ " "	" "

جمــــع ۵۵۰۰۰ کیلو

Contract for caviar purchase in Persian and English. *Courtesy Iron Gate Products, Inc.*

The Russian-European contract is currently held by a Parisian firm, Petrossian. This firm markets the product throughout southern and central Europe and now in the United States.

Germany and the northern-European nations are serviced by a separate contract formerly held by the firm of Dieckmann and Hansen.

W. G. White Ltd. of London holds still another contract for marketing caviar, this one with Iran.

The companies that dominate caviar worldwide are almost all second-, third-, and even fourth- or fifth-generation concerns. A love of caviar and an appreciation for the subtle and complex factors that go into its successful marketing are handed down from father to son, from one caliph to another.

George Fixen comes from a family of caviar merchants. Jacques Nibot has been "adopted" into the line. He has now taken over the operating end of Caviar Volga from Robert Delalagade.

Arnold Hansen-Sturm of Romanoff comes from a long line of men who have made caviar their business—and their life. The firm started when a barrel cooper, Mr. Dieckmann, and a fish wholesaler, Mr. Hansen, joined forces in the free zone of Hamburg, Germany, in the 1850's. They established the first large-scale caviar house in Europe and, because they were in a free zone, were able to import, process, and export without paying duty.

Through marriage, the business melded into the control of one family, and it was a dominant force in the international caviar market until the Russian Revolution of 1917.

Arnold Hansen-Sturm is the fifth generation in the business. He first tasted caviar at the age of two. The father of five children, he terms caviar his family's peanut butter.

As for me, I like to believe that General Malcolm Beyer, whose reputation as one of caviar's memorable caliphs is secure, passed the mantle to me.

Obviously, it takes more than a striving for business success to entice someone into the tenuous, tumultuous world of marketing a dwindling supply of fish eggs to the world. A keenly honed sense of international negotiation is crucial to success. So is being comfortable with the world's most critical gourmets.

But most of all, I think, it is a love of the unusual, the unpredictable, the slightly off-beat that lures us into the business.

As I mentioned in the opening chapter, it is the *mystique* of caviar that holds such appeal for everyone involved—sellers and buyers alike.

ОБЩИЕ УСЛОВИЯ ПОСТАВКИ
GENERAL DELIVERY TERMS

1. Количество

Продавец имеет право поставить проданные по настоящему договору товары до 5 % более или менее от вышеупомянутых количеств.

В зависимости от результата улова и заготовки проданного по настоящему договору товара Продавец имеет право по согласованию с Покупателем заменить один вид товара, обусловленный в настоящем договоре, другим. При отказе Покупателя от такой замены договор в части поставки соответствующего вида товара аннулируется без каких-либо последствий для Продавца.

2. Качество товара

Качество товара, проданного по настоящему договору, должно соответствовать действующим Государственным стандартам СССР, что должно удостоверяться сертификатами о качестве, выданными компетентным на то органом в СССР или заводом-изготовителем.

3. Количественная и качественная сдача-приемка товара

Товар по настоящему договору считается сданным Продавцом и принятым Покупателем:

а) количественно — по весу брутто и количеству мест, указанным в коносаменте, железнодорожной или авианакладной, и по количеству и весу нетто, указанным в спецификации Продавца;

б) по качеству — в соответствии с сертификатом о качестве ,выданным, как это предусмотрено § 2.

Вес брутто и количество мест, указанные в коносаменте, железнодорожной или авианакладной, а также количество и вес нетто, указанные в спецификации Продавца, как и данные по качеству, указанные в спецификации Продавца, как и данные по качеству, указанные в сертификате о качестве согласно § 2, являются окончательными и обязательными для обеих сторон.

4. Арбитраж

Все споры и разногласия, могущие возникнуть из настоящего договора или в связи с ним, подлежат разрешению во Внешнеторговой арбитражной комиссии, решения которой являются окончательными и обязательными для обеих сторон.

Подсудность споров по настоящему договору общим судам исключается.

1. Quantity

The Sellers have the right to deliver the goods sold under the present contract 5% more or less of the abovementioned quantities.

In proportion with the general catch and pack of the goods sold under the present contract the Sellers are entitled with the Buyers consent to replace one kind of goods, stipulated in the present contract, by another one. If the Buyers refuse to accept such replacement the contract in the part of delivery of the corresponding kind of goods is to be cancelled without any consequences for the Sellers.

2. Quality of the Goods

The quality of the goods sold under this contract shall conform to the existing USSR State Standards which must be certified by the certificates of quality issued by the competent organ in the USSR or by the manufacturer.

3. Quantitative and Qualitative Delivery-Acceptance of Goods

The goods to be delivered under the present contract shall be considered as delivered by the Sellers and accepted by the Buyers:

a) as regards the quantity — according to gross weight and number of packages indicated in the Bill of Lading, railroad or airway bill of lading and according to quantity and net weight indicated in the Sellers' specification;

b) as regards the quality — according to the certificate of quality issued as per § 2.

Gross weight and number of packages indicated in the Bill of Lading, railroad or airway bill of lading as well as quantity and net weight indicated in the Sellers' specification and the quality as per § 2 are to be final and binding upon both parties.

4. Arbitration

All disputes and differences which may arise out of this contract or in connection with it are to be settled by the Foreign Trade Arbitration Commission at the USSR Chamber of Commerce, Moscow, in accordance with the rules of this Arbitration Commission whose decisions are final and binding upon both parties to the contract.

Submission of disputes under the present contract to general court is excluded.

Contract for caviar purchase in Russian and English. *Courtesy Iron Gate Products, Inc.*

Specimens of experimental sturgeon grown in captivity in the Soviet Union.

TWELVE

Where Has All the Caviar Gone?

Since buffalo meat never really did catch on as a delicacy, the demise of the mighty American plains animal was not viewed as an epicurean disaster.

But the threatened shortage, and even possible unavailability, of caviar in the future is cause for moans and groans from connoisseurs around the world.

The threat is a serious one despite efforts being made by Iranian and Russian fishing experts to preserve the sturgeon spawning grounds and to create new ones in which fresh generations of sturgeon can grow and contribute their eggs.

The problems have been created by Mother Nature, Father Time, and their offspring and by an industrial society that increases its demands upon nature at a faster rate than nature can provide for.

The problem becomes even more acute because of the concentration of the source of caviar within a small geographical area. About ninety percent of the world's caviar comes from the Caspian Sea. Actually, nearly all sturgeon breed in an area of the Caspian no larger than a thousand acres. This breeding ground is near the mouth of the Volga

River, and even those sturgeon which are caught on the Iranian side of the sea breed in that confined area.

That wouldn't be so bad if Mother Nature were left to her own devices and if Father Time could proceed at his own pace. But intense industrial build-up on the Volga—oil refineries, hydroelectric plants, chemical plants, paper-processing plants, and dams—have siphoned off precious fresh water that would ordinarily have poured into the Caspian, thus aggravating the effect of natural evaporation, which has lowered the sea dramatically over generations.

Caviar production dropped in a serious way when the Russians embarked on their dam-building campaign. One hydroelectric dam followed another along the twenty-three-hundred-mile Volga. Caviar production sank with the Caspian's water level. Production peaked at twenty-three hundred tons in 1936, when the world was just picking itself up from a depression. It sank to fewer than six hundred tons in the early 1970s.

Then, suddenly, there was an increase of available black pearls. Why? It turns out that the Russians had learned to grow fish in hatcheries and then inject them with hormones to make them develop eggs.

According to Cragin R. Whitney, writing in the *International Herald Tribune,* the effort became so intense that in a seven-year period from 1973 through 1979, some 243 million fingerlings were hatched and released into the Caspian.

There is still the problem of insufficient water because of the dams. The power stations stop the flow after the spawning season of March and April. The spawning grounds dry up, the fish eggs end up in the grass, and the birds eat them.

The birds enjoy themselves, and the price of caviar flies higher.

But even with the relative success of the hormone-injection program, the Soviet Union has long expressed concern over the pending shortages of caviar. Not long ago a group of distinguished Soviet intellectuals, including eight biologists, studied the situation and submitted a report that was published in one of Russia's prestigious journals, *Literaturnaya Gazeta.* It was their opinion that unless certain industrial projects on the Volga were halted, the spawning grounds for sturgeon would be reduced from a thousand acres to twenty. They further speculated that attempts being made to create substitute, man-made environments for breeding would eventually fail. The final words from these Soviet intellectuals questioned whether increased hydroelectric capacity was worth losing the pleasure of caviar.

The belly versus big business. The debate still goes on in the Soviet Union. It obviously does not revolve around economics. The exportation of caviar brings in a minuscule amount of revenue, compared with nearly every other industry in Russia. If money could settle the debate, caviar as an industry would come in a dismal last on the priority list.

What complicates things is the Russian love of caviar. Sturgeon is almost a staple on many Russian dinner tables. Its nutritional values are highly regarded by Soviet citizens. But export takes priority where caviar is concerned. And that has meant an acute shortage of caviar within Russia. The shelves are often bare. To take away a bureaucrat's delicacy is one thing, but to strip the proletariat of a favored staple could cause revolution all over again.

So attempts have been made to alleviate the problems. One project undertaken was the building of fish ladders upon which sturgeon could climb over the dams and continue their journey to their spawning grounds.

Until the construction of the ladders, Soviet fishing experts had initiated a program of using boats to transport thousands of sturgeon around dams and had even airlifted them over the dams. Those approaches were expensive and time consuming.

The ladders never really worked either. No one took into consideration the basic nature of the sturgeon, that big, lethargic bottom-feeder of a fish who wouldn't dream of climbing a ladder to get anywhere.

Another scheme instigated by Soviet fishing experts was to crossbreed the beluga sturgeon with the tiny sterlet. The thinking behind this was sound but perhaps over-romantic. By pairing up the beluga, whose sexual drive is low but who carries a large supply of eggs, with the sexually promiscuous sterlet, it was hoped that a sturgeon population explosion would take place. This experiment is still going on and will be for some time. Remember, beluga sturgeon live a long time and take many years before they are capable of breeding. Only time will tell whether a mutual attraction really did take place.

Still another move has been taken within the Soviet Union to increase the sturgeon supply. This involves redirecting parts of the Pechora and Vychegda Rivers so that their fresh waters flow into the Caspian. This takes some doing because the Pechora and Vychegda flow northward. The Caspian is to the south.

The point is that Russia, along with Iran, is cognizant of the real threat that the caviar shortage will worsen, and the Soviets are taking steps to deal with it.

Fingerlings hatched in the experimental station in the U.S.S.R.

Sturgeon fingerling.

One potential solution does not, however, thrill caviar fanciers. Scientists are attempting to perfect artificial caviar. Professor Grigory Slonimsky of the Moscow Academy of Science claims to have created an ersatz caviar that cannot be differentiated from the real thing. Professor Slonimsky toils for the academy's Institute of Elemental Organic Compounds. He created his artificial caviar by converting various proteins to a colloidal state, dissolving them in water, and, to give the concoction texture, adding a fibrous protein. The professor heats the mixture and then pours it into cool vegetable oil. It breaks up into small, round pellets once it's in the oil. The tiny spheres are removed and placed in a vat of tea. The tannic acid in the tea precipitates surface proteins, which form a membrane much like that found in real, honest-to-goodness roe. Finally, the spheres are dyed black, and salt, vitamins, and artificial flavoring are added.

Professor Slonimsky calls his product *iskra.*

Arkady Simonvan, a reporter for the Soviet weekly *Nedelya,* termed the phony fish eggs superb after tasting them in Professor Slonimsky's laboratory.

Production of synthetic caviar has been described to me by Soviet scientists. The machine used to mass produce Professor Slonimsky's discovery is huge. The tiny pellets pop out like ball bearings, each identical with all the others. I mentioned to the Russian in charge of the operation that there was a rumor that the Soviet Union ran out of real caviar eight years ago and that everything they've exported to America has been synthetic.

He smiled.

Just a joke, fellas.

When Arnold Hansen-Sturm was with the Romanoff Caviar Company, he requested of his firm's research-and-development staff that it develop a synthetic caviar that would be superior to that created by the Russians. Mr. Hansen-Sturm viewed the effort as a defensive marketing strategy. He didn't intend for the resulting product to be marketed unless the Soviet Union were to begin marketing its ersatz caviar in America.

The results of Romanoff's efforts proved satisfactory to its president. He claimed that the artificial caviar produced in his laboratories was excellent in taste, texture, and appearance and that it had been produced from natural substances. Moreover, it was said to have a shelf life up to one year, as opposed to a shelf life claimed by the Russians of two weeks.

Another advantage claimed by the Romanoff people for their synthetic caviar is that it is made by machine right within the retail establishment, rather than being manufactured at a central factory and shipped to retail outlets.

There is every possibility that none of us will ever get to sample Romanoff's artificial product. Unless the Soviet Union tried to enter the American market with its synthetic product, Arnold Hansen-Sturm was firm in his position that his product would not be released to the public. And if it was, he saw it as being primarily for use by large catering houses, not by finer restaurants or individual consumers.

Because caviar is so scarce and the price so high, you can imagine the anguish when a shipment of it falls victim to sloppy handling or acts of nature and is lost to the consumer.

One of the most graphic examples of this occurred back in the early sixties. We had purchased a large amount of Iranian caviar from another New York importer. This is often done. In this case, we were trying to beef up a dwindling supply for the upcoming holiday season.

The purchase was delivered to Iron Gate's warehouse in the Foreign Trade Zone of New York, at Stapleton, Staten Island.

I went to Stapleton to inspect the shipment. The odor would have bowled over the bravest of men. The caviar had obviously been in storage for much too long. It was hopelessly spoiled.

I called the other importer and informed him of what our inspection had revealed. He was reluctant to accept our word and, in effect, challenged us.

Never one to mince words, I told the other importer to meet us at the warehouse the following morning at nine sharp. What I didn't tell the man on the other end of the phone was that we wouldn't be alone. We arranged for a U.S. Customs inspector, a Department of Agriculture inspector, and someone from the Food and Drug Administration to accompany us to Stapleton.

We all showed up on time. The decision was unanimous. The caviar was worthless.

"Well, what do you suggest?" asked the importer who'd sold us the shipment.

"It has to be destroyed," the customs agent said.

We walked out on to the dock. The two hundred pounds of caviar that made up the shipment followed us on a hand truck.

We all stood at the edge of the dock and looked into the water below.

"There's nothing else to do with this garbage," the customs man said. "Dump it!"

The hand truck was wheeled to the edge of the pier, and two hundred pounds of what had originally been top-grade caviar was delivered to the briny sea, an expensive gift to whatever fish happened to survive in that polluted water.

It was enough to make a grown caviar lover cry, especially a consumer who has just paid the latest price increase for sturgeon eggs because of the increasing world shortage of the product.

Speaking of shortages—and we do often in our business—political turmoil in Iran has played a major part in increasing the price of caviar. A story circulated around the industry in the spring of 1979 that because of a shutdown of oil production in Iran during the overthrow of the shah, the power plants that drive the refrigeration units had been off for days. According to the reports, more than twenty thousand pounds of prime-grade caviar literally cooked in the blazing Iranian sun.

By the time this book has been published, the veracity of that story will have been verified. There won't be any doubt about about it. The price of caviar on the open market will confirm or deny whether all that caviar did, in fact, rot in the sun. If it did, the loss of twenty thousand pounds will shoot the price of beyond what normal world shortages would have caused. If there was ever a classic example of supply and demand at work to shape an economic market, caviar is it. It's right out of a textbook.

Hauling in a sturgeon on the Hudson River.

THIRTEEN

The Hudson—Caspian West?

There was a time not long ago when the United States was a major contributor to the world caviar market.

In 1859, Ferdinand Hansen, of the firm of Dieckmann and Hansen, now known as the Romanoff Caviar Company, was sent from Europe to America to buy caviar for export to Europe. At that time, the Delaware and Penn Grove Rivers were producing sizable quantities of sturgeon roe, and most of it was exported.

Industrialization and overfishing soon put an end to America's sturgeon and caviar industry, just as they threaten to do to Russia's fishing fleets along the Volga.

But the question is now being asked whether there exists the possibility of reviving America's sturgeon and caviar industry. As far as William Dovel is concerned, the answer is a resounding *yes*.

Bill Dovel is a marine biologist. He graduated from the University of Maryland and served with a U.S. army biological-warfare unit. Upon his discharge, a friend suggested that he apply for a job with an agency charged with the management of the Chesapeake Bay. He applied, was hired, and for twelve years studied the estuarine patterns of that large and complex waterway. In the process, he began to develop his own unorthodox and slightly irreverent approach to marine research. A craftsman as well as a scientist, he invented a myriad of devices to aid in his research efforts. He's also a talented marine illustrator, and many of the reports he published based upon his work were illustrated with his own drawings.

In 1972, Dovel moved to New York and began a three-year study of sturgeon in the Hudson River. It was a state-funded project that involved an eighty-mile stretch of that river—from the mouth, near the Statue of Liberty, to Poughkeepsie, New York. He traveled up and down those eighty miles in a houseboat that he had converted into an elaborate research trawler and into which he incorporated many of his own inventions.

A key to the success of Dovel's sturgeon research revolved around the rapport he developed with the river's commercial fishermen. Soon, these crusty, independent, and slightly suspicious gentlemen began calling Bill whenever they caught a particularly large sturgeon. Simultaneously, he began tagging sturgeon in the river and even attached transmitters to some of the fish so that they could be tracked day by day.

In the three years of Bill Dovel's work in the Hudson, he tagged almost five thousand sturgeon. Calls began coming in from children, housewives, and pleasure fishermen who ran across sturgeon with Dovel's tiny red tags. The address on the tags also began generating letters. Based upon these responses, elaborate maps and charts were created into which tiny pins were inserted to chart the migratory patterns of these creatures of the deep.

The end result was a systematic view of how sturgeon travel and spawn in the Hudson.

"I'm more interested in the *system* than most scientists," Dovel says. "The individual parts are fascinating, of course, but it is an overall understanding of any waterway system that reaps the sort of results that can be translated into tangible action."

He goes on to say, based upon his Hudson River project, "There's no doubt in my mind that sturgeon fishing could be nurtured and developed into a major industry in New York—provided, of course, that the appropriate governmental agencies take the necessary steps to effectively manage the estuarine systems of the region. You can't begin to manage such a system until you truly understand it."

Harold Hansen-Sturm agrees with Bill Dovel that the answer to the caviar crunch might well be found right here at home.

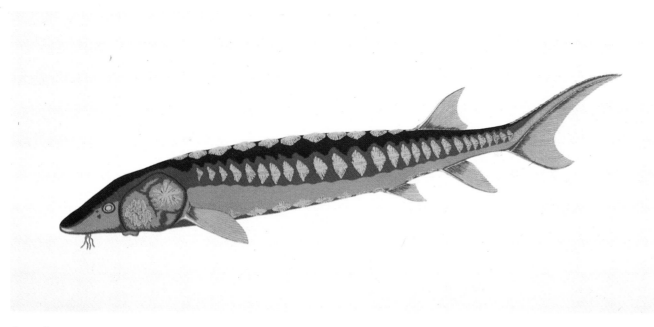

American sturgeon.

"The potentials of developing a sturgeon industry in New York's Hudson River are very strong," says Hansen-Sturm. "I feel that the United States will become very prominent in the international caviar market, along with other areas of the world besides Iran and Russia."

Romanoff, Iron Gate, and others are actively exploring the globe in search of new sources. Romanoff in particular has shifted emphasis from the more expensive sturgeon caviar to whitefish, lumpfish, and salmon. Iceland sells large amounts of lumpfish roe. The Great Lakes area provides an abundance of whitefish. The bulk of salmon roe comes from the West Coast of the United States.

"Romanoff was the first importer of Icelandic lumpfish roe," says Arnold Hansen-Sturm. "We started marketing it forty years ago. And right now, lumpfish caviar surpasses all other caviar in amounts sold throughout the world."

According to researcher Bill Dovel, there are between twenty-two and twenty-five species of sturgeon in the world, with five of them being very much at home in United States waters.

"The quality of sturgeon found right here in the Hudson River is as good as that found in the Volga River and in the Caspian Sea," says Dovel. "After all, fish are what they eat. The quality of meat and roe reflects the feeding patterns of the animal. Most sturgeon feeding on our East Coast takes place in the ocean. Once the sturgeon leave U.S.

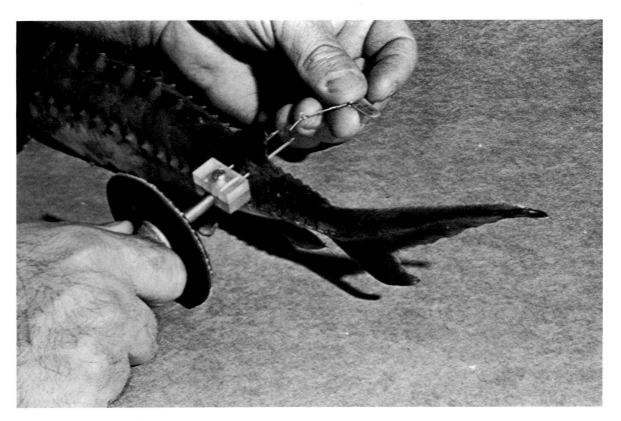

Tagging a sturgeon.

waters, they become easy fishing for foreign fleets. What's needed is a concerted, reasoned plan, probably a ten-year plan in which our coastal waters can be placed under management based upon knowledge. Until that time, a valuable resource is being lost to us."

Iran and the Soviet Union don't have a problem with managing the waters in which sturgeon mature. The estuarine system in those countries is contained. But here in the United States, the system involves many rivers, many states. What Dovel is calling for, and has lobbied for with state and federal officials, is an integrated plan of action.

"We don't have the laws to protect the sturgeon," he says. "Nobody even knows how many sturgeon there are in the Hudson. Fishermen dump caviar into the river every day because a caviar industry hasn't been formulated. Most fishermen sell to individuals and don't keep records. The current law says that sturgeon can't be fished from the channels. That means the sturgeon easily escape to the oceans, where other countries fish them."

Based upon his research, Bill Dovel estimates that male sturgeon stay in the Hudson River system for about three or four years. Female sturgeon remain in the system for eight to ten years. It takes about twelve years for a male sturgeon to mature, eighteen to twenty years for a female.

"With a well-thought-out management plan, these fish can be caught by American fishermen and can satisfy the needs of the consumer, including the consumer of caviar," Dovel says.

Only recently have those of us in the business of providing caviar to the American consumer turned our attention to the potentials of such resources as the Hudson River and to the sort of research being provided by William Dovel. It isn't an industry effort. At Iron Gate, we are now helping fund Dovel's continuing research efforts. Romanoff is do-

A sturgeon net in the Hudson.

Taking sturgeon from the nets.

A sturgeon on the Hudson dock.

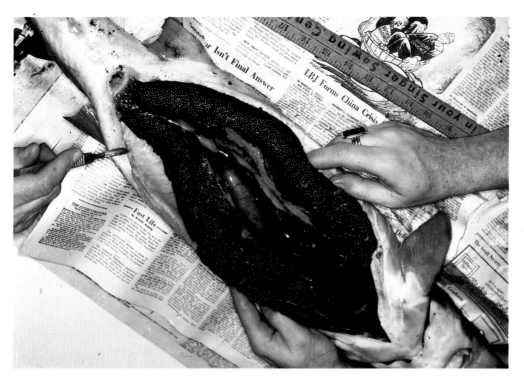

Taking roe from a Hudson sturgeon.

ing the same. But even though it's being done on an individual basis, everyone will benefit from the results.

The prognosis for caviar availability and prices in the future is mixed. Personally, I feel that the supply will increase and therefore lower prices of the expensive types—beluga, sevruga, and osetra. Arnold Hansen-Sturm isn't quite as optimistic.

George Fixen, who heads up Panacaviar, Inc., the firm that held the exclusive Iranian caviar contract for the United States until 1979, is well aware of the factors that go into the supply-and-demand formula for caviar. It was his view that the spring 1979 catch of osetra and sevruga would be, at least, normal. That would mean no increase in prices.

However forecasting caviar prices is like forecasting the weather, but even worse. The variables are many and fragile. Nature's laws are fickle and unpredictable. Man refuses to heed the warning not to "mess around with Mother Nature."

Even religion plays a role in determining the price of caviar.

The new government of Iran, know as the revolutionary council, derives much of its power from the Muslim religion it serves. And one of the first acts of the council after gaining power in Iran was to ban the eating of sturgeon because the fish does not have scales.

Hebrew laws of *kashrut* also prohibit eating any fish without scales.

But does the sturgeon have scales?

Evidently no one, including the new government leaders of Iran, has a definitive answer. It wasn't long after Iran's revolutionary council banned the eating of sturgeon that the prime minister, Mehdi Bazargan, rescinded the council's ban. For caviar lovers in other parts of the globe, the prime minister's action was bad news. If Muslims are allowed to eat sturgeon and, of course, sturgeon roe, it will mean less caviar available for export.

"There will always be a question about whether sturgeon have scales," says marine biologist Bill Dovel. "It depends upon the perspective from which you view it. From a purely scientific point of view, the sturgeon could be said to have scales. From a cultural or religious point of view, it might not."

Traditionally, a fish was checked for scales by drawing a piece of silk across it from head to tail. If the silk caught, the assumption was that there were scales of sufficient development to consider the fish acceptable to Muslim and Jewish dietary laws.

"I'd never heard of the silk-fabric test," says Dovel, "but it seems to me it wouldn't be definitive. Juvenile sturgeon have small, tough barbs that disappear toward the time they spawn. Silk would catch on those barbs but would probably slide over the smooth skin of a mature fish."

Other fish taken from the Hudson.

James P. McCaffrey, president of Romanoff's parent company, Iroquois Grocery Products, Inc. Romanoff is the largest distributor of domestic caviar in the United States.

Dovel also points out that the sturgeon's ancestors were possessed of a type of armor plate. Over the past 250 million years that plate turned into modified scales of the sort found on shad and striped bass, as well as on sturgeon as we know them today. According to Dovel, sturgeon have five rows of plates that could be considered modified scales. And, he says, there are even smaller scales in between that are known as dentines.

What Iran's ruling body determines in the near future about whether that nation's Muslim citizens will be allowed to consume sturgeon and its roe will have a definite effect upon the price of caviar worldwide. And if America's Hebrew leaders decide that caviar is kosher, that will increase domestic demand and could even further boost prices.

In the meantime, Bill Dovel's painstaking research into the life of Hudson River sturgeon goes on, this time with funding from the caviar giants rather than from the government agencies that supported his previous work.

"With the proper research efforts into the Hudson's estuarine system, and some creative lawmaking, there's no doubt in my mind that we might soon be eating quality caviar that didn't have to be shipped from Iran or from the Soviet Union. It could be trucked in a matter of hours from the river to New York City's finest restaurants," says Dovel.

All I can say as someone in the business of providing good caviar to the consumer is that we all wish Bill Dovel well and hope that the funding we're able to provide him eases the pressure we all face in trying to help caviar supply meet caviar demand, at a price that doesn't limit the enjoyment of this delicacy to only the richest customers.

FOURTEEN

And Even Farther West...

One of the wonderful things about a free-enterprise system is that a shortage of anything generally creates an industry dedicated to filling the gap.

The caviar shortage and the resulting high prices have piqued the interest of many entrepreneurs, including such people as Mats and Daphne Engstrom of San Francisco.

The Engstroms became interested in marketing caviar from sturgeon caught in West Coast waters a few years ago when they first heard that sturgeon existed there. They began to experiment, and through trial and error, and by delving into all available material written on caviar production, they were able to produce a black caviar that caused even such an acknowledged gourmet as the *New York Times* food expert Craig Claiborne to rave about its taste. Mr. Claiborne said, "The Engstroms' most recently made caviar . . . was outstanding in texture and flavor. I would place it in competition with any imported caviar sold in this country from no matter where."

Because the laws of California prohibit fishing for sturgeon as anything but game fish, the roe used by this enterprising couple from the

West Coast must be obtained from commercial fishermen in Oregon and Washington.

The Engstroms produce little caviar and market it only to personal friends at about a hundred dollars a pound. Their major income is derived from the processing of Dungeness crab, salmon, and crayfish, with crayfish the big moneymaker.

But they see a future in caviar derived from America's waters, just as at the turn of the century. Whether California holds more potential than New York's Hudson River remains to be seen. The important point is that no one is taking Iranian and Russian caviar for granted any longer. Caviar will always be one of the world's most treasured taste treats, and those engaged in providing it to anxious palates are looking beyond the Volga and the Caspian.

FIFTEEN

A Tasting

I've hosted numerous caviar tastings, the menus of some of which are contained in this book.

The first tasting I ever conducted was at the home of Mr. and Mrs. Roger Yaseen. Roger Yaseen is head of the United States division of the Confrérie de la Chaîne des Rôtisseurs. The tasting was sponsored by the New York Wine and Food Society, and twenty-five guests came to enjoy the varied menu of caviar.

Since then, caviar tastings have become a part of my life and the lives of others in the business of providing caviar to discriminating consumers.

I've hosted tastings at the University Club of Phoenix, the U.N. Plaza, the Rainbow Grill high atop the RCA Building, the Swiss Chalet in San Juan, Puerto Rico, and numerous private homes. The guests include a Who's Who of gastronomic expertise. Many of them fly in from Europe to attend a tasting. Once, the gathering was graced with a surprise visit by Xavier Hermes Girrard and his brother. Mr. Girrard owns the famed Paris department store Hermes.

George Moran, former vice-president of Manufacturer's Hanover, has flown from Palm Beach to attend a caviar tasting.

Bollinger Brut 1973

Ayala Brut 1970

Aalborg Jubilaeums Akvavit

Chandon Cuvée de Pinot Noir
Napa Valley

Hennessey Bras d'Or

Scotch Salmon
+
Salmon Red Caviar
+
Russian Sevruga
Iranian Sevruga
+
Pressed Iranian
+
Fresh Iranian Sevruga
+
Fresh Iranian Osetra
+
Fresh Iranian Beluga
+
Lake Sturgeon
Chocolate Roll

A menu, from a caviar tasting held at the home of Mr. and Mrs. William Lembeck. Mrs. Lembeck, a noted wine expert, teaches a wine course at the Waldorf-Astoria.

Of course, a reputation must precede these tastings to induce people to travel to them. The caviar must be of excellent quality; the vodka, the best and properly chilled; the champagne, of good vintage, and everything must be served with appropriate good taste and splendor.

I can only suggest for those of you who are always on the lookout for a new and better party idea that you try your own personal caviar tasting, It's easy as long as you buy good quality and take the time and interest to serve whatever variety of caviar you choose in as elegant and proper a setting as is humanly possible.

I know one thing: Your friends will never forget it.

The photographs in this book illustrating a recent caviar tasting demonstrate how the occasion quickly becomes festive. Among my quests were William Gaines, the publisher of *Mad* magazine; Anne P. Griffiths; John C. Bruno, owner of New York's Pen & Pencil Restaurant: Lyle Stuart and Carole Livingston, my publisher and editor; labor negotiator Theodore W. Kheel; friends Mr. and Mrs. Murray Hillman;

Ms. Maj Kalfus; Helga A. Phillippe; Burton Greenberg; René and Elsa Aponte of Puerto Rico; and my daughter Elisabeth.

Naturally, with a caviar tasting you build toward the best. We started with fresh whitefish roe, fresh salmon roe, and pasteurized salmon roe, all three served on one plate. These are all orange and looked very appealing. We drank Stolichnaya vodka that had been frozen in a cake of ice.

Fresh North American sturgeon caviar followed, along with more vodka, and the evening got merrier. When we moved on the Russian pasteurized sevruga and Russian fresh sevruga, we switched to Taitinger champagne.

000 beluga. *Photo: Lonny Kalfus.*

Next came Russian fresh osetra caviar with more champagne—this time Dom Pérignon. Some of us were in a state of bliss by now, because the osetra is truly a wonderful experience.

The climax was a tin of 000 beluga and the final drops of the Dom Pérignon.

I can assure you, we were a happy and satisfied group at the close of the evening.

Setting up a tasting, Jerry Stein opens up a tin of 000 beluga, flanked by pasteurized salmon roe (upper left), pasteurized sevruga (upper right), fresh salmon roe and fresh whitefish roe (lower left), and fresh sevruga (lower right). *Photo: Lonny Kalfus.*

The first caviars are arranged on each plate: fresh whitefish roe, fresh salmon roe, and pasteurized salmon roe. *Photo: Lonny Kalfus.*

Caviar ready to be brought to the table. *Photo: Lonny Kalfus.*

(Opposite page) Carole Livingston and Jerry Stein at rear of table before the guests are seated. On the table with some of the caviar, are Dom Pérignon and Taitinger champagnes and Stolichnaya vodka frozen in ice. *Photo: Lonny Kalfus.*

The tasting begins. *Photo: Lonny Kalfus.*

Mr. and Mrs. René Aponte of Puerto Rico enjoy fresh Russian sevruga. *Photo: Lonny Kalfus.*

Eagerly awaiting the service of fresh Russian beluga, facing the camera from left to right: Elisabeth Stein, Burton Greenberg, John Bruno (looking away), Marilyn Hillman, Murray Hillman. *Photo: Lonny Kalfus.*

Happy tasters finishing up. Left side of table, front to rear: Maj Kalfus, Burton Greenberg, John Bruno (obscured), Marilyn Hillman, Murray Hillman (obscured), Lyle Stuart, Carole Livingston (obscured). Right side of table, front to rear: Theodore W. Kheel, William Gaines, Anne P. Griffiths, Jerry Stein, René Aponte, Elsa V. Aponte. *Photo: Lonny Kalfus.*

Maj Kalfus watches as beluga is served. *Photo: Lonny Kalfus.*

An extravagance of excess: Theodore W. Kheel is spoon fed beluga caviar by Elisabeth Stein. *Photo: Lonny Kalfus.*

Caviar as served at the world-famous Maxim's, Paris. *Photo courtesy Maxim's.*

SIXTEEN

Serving Caviar

Caviar connoisseurs love to debate the relative merits of various types of caviar. But they love even more to debate how best to serve the black berries from the Caspian Sea.

Every lover of caviar has his or her favorite serving suggestion. I do too. But all I can do is present to you a compilation of the most popular of these suggestions and my own admittedly prejudiced choices, then encourage you to experiment, improvise, create, and come up with your own favorite way of enjoying caviar that will become your contribution to the debate.

Few gourmets will argue strenuously against the belief that top-quality, whole-grain caviar, be it beluga, osetra, or sevruga, is best enjoyed *au naturel.* The unique, memorable flavor of fresh, whole berries doesn't need any embellishment. A gleaming mound of beluga malossol in a pretty serving dish surrounded by crushed ice is all anyone with a palate should need. Some even serve it directly from the tin in which it was purchased, to avoid disturbing the berries.

But even with a generally unanimous agreement on the merits of enjoying good caviar in its natural state, debate still exists over such

things as the proper utensil to use when eating it, the right liquid re-
freshment to sip with it, and what foods should not be served alongside
it.

My own preference is a wooden tongue depressor, of the type used
by physicians when they tell you to open wide and say "Ahhhhhh!"

Why a wooden utensil? Well, I consider it almost a crime to use silver
because of how easily it tarnishes. Besides, metal of any sort is an active
substance. It responds to food eaten from it. I hate to think of anything
altering, even minutely, the purity of good caviar. Yes, this might be
nothing more than a psychological response on my part, as it is with
others who share my view. But isn't caviar, after all, more than reality?
Isn't using elegant serving pieces for any food a psychological indulgence? Much of the mystique of enjoying good food is psychological.

At any rate, having a neat pile of tongue depressors next to your
caviar bowl is bound to elicit comments, especially if some of your
guests are physicians.

I've also served caviar on spoons made of bone, tortoise, mother-of-
pearl, and horn. Just as long as it isn't silver. I'd even go as far as to
suggest saving up the little plastic spoons given you with your take-out
soup at the deli. Some of the most sophisticated connoisseurs I know
serve caviar with these spoons.

Most people prefer something with their caviar. For some, it involves
mixing it with other foods. Others simply need a base upon which to
spoon the caviar.

A piece of thin, freshly made toast is a favorite of some. Some say
butter should not be used because if the caviar is of good enough quality, its own natural fat should be enough to moisten the toast. But as in
any debate, there is an opposing viewpoint. There are those who feel
that butter adds to caviar's taste and who further insist upon a squeeze
of lemon over the caviar to mitigate its oiliness. I use lemon juice when
eating caviar that has been more heavily salted than the best grades, but
I find that it gets in the way of the taste of really good caviar.

Another way some people enjoy their caviar is to sprinkle some finely
chopped onions, hard-boiled-egg yolks or whites, or chives on it. Again,
the addition of these ingredients can spruce up a caviar of less than top
quality, but the *au naturel* approach is still, by far, the best when really
fine caviar is served.

Toast isn't the only base for caviar. Black bread, the Russian favorite,
is excellent. Caviar is served at various tables on French bread, pumpernickel, plain crackers, rye toast, or, as some Russians are reputed to
serve it, on cucumber slices.

A traditionally styled caviar service in Baccarat crystal. *Photo: Jean-Michel Kollar, courtesy Baccarat Crystal.*

Another Baccarat caviar service, in a more modern style. *Photo courtesy Baccarat Crystal.*

The blini, a Russian buckwheat pancake, has always been a favorite vehicle for caviar. Often, pressed caviar is rolled in blinis, with sour cream as a popular addition.

If you decide to use crackers with the caviar you serve, be sure to buy bland, unsalted ones. Since salt is such an important part of caviar's processing and eventual taste, to add more than was deemed appropriate by the master blender would be sacrilege.

Caviar is also good when used to fill a hole cut out of a boiled or baked new potato. It's also delicious when used in jellied soups or in cold borscht.

Now that the point has presumably been made about the joys of eating good caviar without adornment, let's discuss a more common situation.

Most caviar is garnished with other foods. You seldom find a caviar bowl on a serving table that does not have within easy proximity bowls of chopped hard-boiled-egg yolks and whites, onions, chives, capers, olives, pimiento slivers, butter, cream cheese, and sour cream, Here again, the individual palate must reign supreme. There's no doubt that the taste sensations that can be created by combining caviar with some of the above foods are succulent and should be experienced. I know someone who says that the ultimate taste sensation is caviar combined

A typical caviar service.

Caviar service at the Breakers Hotel, Palm Beach. Left to right: Executive chef Manfred Hacker, wearing his medal of the Academy of Chefs; Henry Warren, C.H.A., wearing the distinguished medal of the International Wine and Food Society; and *garde manger* Francisco Lopez, with his Five Star Award emblem. *Photo courtesy the Breakers.*

with finely chopped shallots, with a dash of cayenne pepper. (Certain gourmets also enjoy it with coarse black pepper.)

There is a very exclusive club that meets in Switzerland during the prime caviar months of May, June, October, and November. It's called the Beluga Club. The members of this organization are strict adherents of eating caviar in its most natural state. Anyone in the club who would be gauche enough to sprinkle egg yolks or onions on fresh beluga is almost automatically banished for life.

The club will tolerate a tiny drop of lemon or a dash of black pepper but nothing more. However, if you must add something to your caviar, make it a freshly baked Idaho potato. That's right, a baked potato. That legendary gourmand Diamond Jim Brady often ordered in his favorite New York restaurants a baked potato stuffed with fresh beluga caviar. That was when you could buy beluga as cheaply as a stein of beer.

And by the way, Diamond Jim knew a good thing when he tasted it. Caviar sprinkled on a baked potato, with or without sour cream, is delicious.

The Russians, who view caviar in a slightly more everyday manner than Americans, are particularly fond of heaping it on a buckwheat blini, then sprinkling finely chopped onions and hard-boiled eggs over it and covering everything with a mound of extremely thick sour cream.

See? Everyone has a favorite way of serving and eating caviar.

There is another exclusive caviar club. This one is called the Nobles' Club, and its headquarters is in Riga, in the Soviet Union. Here, among the gourmets, the ultimate taste treat is to take the breast meat of a cold roast pheasant and to mince it very fine. It mustn't be ground; a knife should be used.

Each club member heaps as much fresh beluga caviar as he wishes onto a thin slice of black bread. Then, the minced pheasant breast is sprinkled over the caviar. Only the amount of meat that naturally adheres to the caviar is used. It's never piled on.

Frances Parkinson Keyes was fond of caviar soufflés.

Robert Campbell, of W. G. White Ltd., Britain's oldest importer of caviar, reportedly preferred to smear caviar on the back of his hand and lick it off, much as Mexicans enjoy licking salt after a shot of tequila.

The politician and gourmet Clement Freud supposedly finishes off a tin of fresh caviar every morning for breakfast.

Some gourmets prefer their caviar on half-inch slices of toasted Italian bread, buttered with sweet butter and garnished with finely chopped shallots and a little lemon juice.

Others like their Beluga on toast with chopped parsley, gherkins, and remoulade sauce.

For still others, a truffled pâté is a must with their caviar.

There are, of course, an infinite variety of dishes that are enhanced by the addition of caviar. Some of them are contained in the recipes in this book. When concocting your own combinations, however, one rule of thumb should be followed: It generally works best when the caviar, with its wholly unique and distinctive taste, is combined with relatively bland foods that benefit from an injection of flavor. Such delicate foods as sea food, turkey, artichokes, cottage cheese, eggs, sour cream, and avocados truly come to life with caviar's zesty flavor.

Small boiled new potatoes filled with caviar and garnished with sour cream, as served at Chasen's, Los Angeles. *Photo courtesy Chasen's.*

Caviar service at New York's famed Palace Restaurant. *Photo courtesy the Palace.*

Here are some simple ideas using caviar.

   ... use it as a topping for broiled fish.

   ... top off a jellied madrilene with a dab of caviar.

   ... mix cream cheese with red caviar (salmon roe) and stuff it into celery or artichoke hearts.

   ... sprinkle some whole-grain caviar on egg salad.

   ... stuff mushroom crowns with caviar, either red or black—or use both for an even more tempting visual appeal on your appetizer tray.

   ... make a caviar omelet.

   ... mix pressed caviar with cream cheese and serve on buttered toast fingers.

   ... mold a ball of cream cheese and spread with pressed caviar. Cut into wedges.

   ... one of my very favorite uses of caviar is in homemade dressing. The addition of a generous amount of whole-grain caviar to fine wine vinegar and top-quality olive oil gives this dressing a unique and exciting flavor. But don't use it with anything but plain greens. A mixed salad is simply too strong in itself and will clash with the caviar dressing.

MY FAVORITE NEW YEAR'S EVE

   In 1968 it snowed heavily on New Year's Eve. My wife and I were forced to limit the number of parties we attended. The first one was our own, and we served caviar and champagne until everyone departed for the next celebration.

   We managed to make one more party and stayed at it until after four in the morning. We then carefully made our way along slippery country roads toward our home. As we passed the home of friends who'd had their own party, we noticed that a bedroom light was on upstairs.

   "Let's stop in and say hello," I suggested.

   Our friends were getting ready for bed and were in their robes.

   "Come in," they said, "and have a nightcap."

   We sat in their living room and sipped champagne. The conversation came around to food, and the lady of the house mentioned that the crepes suzette she'd attempted for the party had failed.

Caviar service at the Peninsula Hotel, Hong Kong. *Photo: CLIC Studios Ltd.*

My wife makes wonderful crepes, and the two women headed for the kitchen for a fling at creating a new batch based upon my wife's technique.

It wasn't long before a superbly concocted batch of crepes was placed on a coffee table in the living room. Naturally, the next question was what ingredients should be used to fill them.

"Tell you what," I said. "I have some caviar left over from the party. I'll go get it."

There were many protests about my making the half-mile drive in that weather, but I insisted.

I returned with the caviar, and at 5:30 in the morning the four of us sat on the floor, my wife and I in dinner clothes, our friends still in their robes. We feasted on caviar crepes, savored the chilled champagne, watched the sun come up, and agreed it was the most pleasurable New Year's Eve any of us had ever spent.

The four of us have been spending it that way ever since.

Speaking of caviar crepes, the great caterer-chef Rudy Stanish is literally the creator of the buffet omelette and crepe. He often uses caviar purchased from us at Iron Gate. Rudy Stanish and caviar omelets are synonymous.

These are just a few simple uses of caviar. The variations are limitless, and although certain combinations of foods with these delectable black pearls might seem bizarre to some, it's your taste buds that count. Experiment—it's one of the true joys of cooking. And who knows? You might create a caviar dish that will become a staple in the finest restaurants in the world.

We now turn to the next area of debate among caviar lovers, and that has to do with the perfect alcoholic beverage to accompany their favorite food.

There are two main favorites—dry vintage champagne and vodka.

The champagne advocates feel that any alcoholic drink stronger than wine abuses the palate and renders it less capable of fully enjoying the caviar taste.

Vodka proponents disagree and defend their choice on two counts—tradition and what they claim is a unique taste combination when sturgeon roe and potato-based vodka combine in the mouth.

I enjoy caviar with both champagne and vodka.

(Opposite page) At Tony's, in Houston, caviar is shown as served in an antique English silver crab (about 1860). *Photo: Kaye Marvins.*

I've recently changed the approach at the caviar tastings I conduct around the country. I'm not sure that any alcoholic beverage should be consumed prior to tasting fine caviar. The French have always known that anything but wine dulls the palate and should not be imbibed before enjoying a good meal. The same principle would hold true with caviar.

If vodka is your preference, it should be served in shot glasses that are nestled in crushed ice. Nothing but thoroughly chilled vodka will

Caviar at the Maisonette, Cincinnati. Garnishes shown, left to right, are chopped parsley, egg whites, egg yolks, and onion. *Photo: Keller Studios.*

do. It can be pink, yellow, or white vodka, and filling the shot glasses with a pre-mixed, extra-dry vodka martini is acceptable. True purists insist upon Latvian vodka whose 120-proof kick provides a perfect slow burn to complement caviar's gentle taste. And many of these same purists will add a dash of freshly ground black pepper to their vodka. It represents the ultimate authenticity, they claim.

For champagne advocates, only the dryest will do. Champagne taken with caviar should be brut or extra-sec. The dryness of champagne has

Obviously enjoying themselves at a caviar party are (left to right): Carole Livingston, Jerry Stein, Marlies Jung, Lyle Stuart, Anne Griffiths, Bill Gaines, Charles Stein (on floor), Marianne Stein, Button (the dog), and Diane Stein. *Photo: Elisabeth Stein*.

At an impromptu caviar party, Elisabeth Stein feeds a caviar hero to *Mad* magazine's Bill Gaines (right) and publisher Lyle Stuart. *Photo: Marlies Jung*.

Just a few of the goodies at the caviar party. *Photo: Marlies Jung*.

to do with the amount of sugar added to it. The following is a simple guide to judging the relative dryness of champagnes.

FRENCH	AMERICAN	SUGAR CONTENT
brut	natural (very, very dry)	½–1½%
extra-sec	extra dry	1–2%
sec	dry	2–4%
demi-sec	semi-sweet	4–6%
doux	sweet	more than 6%

The most frequently ordered champagne in fine restaurants to go with a serving of caviar is Dom Pérignon, the leader in the Moët et Chandon line. Vintages are a matter of personal choice, but the excellent 1970 seems perfect with beluga malossol. Taitinger, too, has been popular, and so has vintage Krug. But again, personal preferences, as well as the pocketbook, dictate the choice you make. And you might keep in mind the philosophy that most experienced drinkers have about mixing expensive brands of liquor with run-of-the-mill mixers. There's no sense in specifying Beefeater gin to go into a Tom Collins. The same holds true when eating second-line caviar. A brut Dom Pérignon is wasted on less than top-quality caviar.

Turbot with whitefish roe. *Photo: Marlies Jung.*

Serving the turbot. *Photo: Marlies Jung.*

Enjoying caviar and Krug Champagne at "21" are (left to right) Jerry Berns, co-owner of "21"; Remy Krug, director of Krug Champagne; and Jerry Stein.

The choice is yours. When in doubt, choose elegance and style when serving caviar. As it becomes more precious, more in demand, rarer, more unavailable, it requires even greater reverence if it is to be enjoyed completely. Crystal and china bowls of it packed in crushed ice are the appropriate settings for glistening black sturgeon berries. Good vodka chilled to a frigid temperature and swallowed immediately behind the succulent sturgeon roe is altogether proper and right.

Good caviar and good champagne or good vodka. Made for each other.

Don't just serve caviar; present it, It's entirely worth it.

SEVENTEEN

The Ultimate Chic?

Only a city in love with elegance could support a series of restaurants devoted exclusively to the sale of caviar.

What other city could that be except Paris?

In Paris, the noontime diner has a choice of such spots. He simply drops in, orders from a wide variety of caviar available on the menu, and either sits at one of the six to sixteen small tables or leans on the counter and enjoys a beluga or osetra luncheon while reading the newspaper, a glass of chilled vodka or champagne at his side.

It's sort of a caviar Nedick's, with obvious differences. *Vive la différence!*

These Parisian caviar restaurants dot the city. They're usually no bigger than forty by twenty feet. The tables are small.

There's a fine caviar restaurant on rue Madeleine. It's called Caviar Caspia, and it's owned and operated by the marketing firm of that name.

And of course, there's Robert Delalagade's La Maison du Caviar, where the tablecloths and napkins are paper.

The ultimate chic.

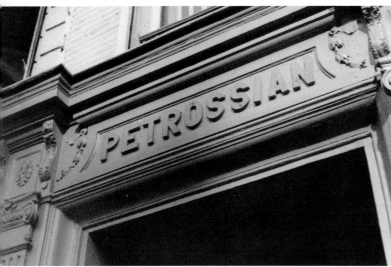

Various elegant Paris restaurants noted (among other things) for their caviar.

Paris's answer to Brink's: caviar-delivery
wagons.

George Kinzler, creator of Macy's Cellar in New York, stands in front of the caviar
display.

Fauchon, Paris.

Robert Delalagade (right) and managing
director Jacques Nebot, in front of their
Maison du Caviar.

The elegant brass on the door of Maison du Caviar.
Photo: Carole Livingston.

Caviar-stuffed eggs. *Photos: Marlies Jung.*

EIGHTEEN

A Guide to Goodness

My hometown of New York City doesn't do badly by those succulent little black pearls.

The following list is almost a random one—for there are many other fine restaurants.

My father-in-law, Jerry Berns, would cut me into small pieces if I didn't lead the list with his own 21 Club, the class caviar lovers' meeting-place. Probably more of us gather there than at any other watering hole in the world. This celebrity-packed restaurant is, of course, at 21 West 52nd Street (212-583-7200).

For sheer elegance, Frank Valenza's Palace is considered the gold-cup winner. The Palace is easily one of the most expensive dining places in America (if not *the* most expensive). Valenza does things for the preparation and serving of caviar that add to the pleasure of its taste. The Palace is at 420 East 59th Street (212-355-5150).

La Folie has style. *Cue* magazine recently cited it as winning high marks "for sheer flash and glitter." Here, for a price, you can heap caviar onto hot blinis or toast and then select from five "garnitures," graciously served on imported china. La Folie is at 21 East 61st Street (212-765-1400).

It is said that the Russian Tea Room boasts the widest caviar selection in Manhattan. This theatrical hangout also boasts a choice of seventeen imported vodkas to go with it. This restaurant is at 150 West 57th Street (212-265-0947).

The Carlyle Restaurant has a more sophisticated flavor. You might observe Jackie Onassis lunching with a Doubleday author at one table, while across the room Warren Beatty and Robert Redford sit at adjoining tables. The Carlyle specializes in beluga, both in its restaurant and in its adjacent Gallery. The latter is an intimate area furnished with cozy couches and attractive green plants. The Carlyle is at 35 East 76th Street (212-744-1600).

When you scout for fine caviar in New York City, you will find your own oasis, I'm sure.

We can't talk about Paris and New York and ignore London.

While there, journey to the Caviar Bar Restaurant. This is situated in Knightsbridge, a few blocks from Harrods. It's owned by a young British lord, Viscount Richard Newport. There is nothing in the window so gauche as a menu or a credit-card sticker, though credit cards are accepted. The decor is black and white, and even including the seats at the tiny bar, the restaurant can accommodate only thirty-three people at a time. It has been reported that Lord Newport now serves as much as a ton of caviar each year. There are four kinds of caviar available, though beluga is easily the favorite.

One advantage of such large use of caviar at the caviar bar is that none of it sits for very long in the air. Therefore, there is no oxidizing effect such as afflicts the caviar served at some other restaurants.

The Caviar Bar Restaurant is at 22, Brompton Road, SW1 (01-589-8772).

NINETEEN

Is Caviar Good for You?

For years the Russians have claimed that caviar is among the most nutritious foods in the world. Some claim that sevruga cures impotence; some say that osetra contributes to bowel regularity; and so on.

I've heard claims that caviar contains forty nutrients, making it the world's most beneficial natural food.

Remember that the early Persians called caviar *chav-jar,* or "cake of strength." They believed it had potent curing powers.

The Brain Research Foundation once did a study of caviar's nutrition. They identified some forty-seven vitamins and minerals, including a substance called acetylcholine, an important nervous-system chemical.

Part of the Brain Research Foundation's study dealt with the relative value of foods in staving off hangovers. The foundation studied thirty-five volunteer medical students and concluded that acetylcholine produced a greater tolerance for alcohol. By extension, that could mean that caviar also has that beneficial effect. A *New York Times* reporter who covered the foundation's findings concluded that caviar is "why caviar-eating Russians show a notable capacity for alcohol."

There have also been claims that caviar is a prime aphrodisiac. No one has ever come up with scientific proof of this, but the chances are that if anyone could ever prove that caviar was an aphrodisiac, you'd find sturgeon breeding in every backyard in America. The caviar industry would rival the automotive industry. And maybe the cold war would be a thing of the past.

One final note about caviar's nutritional value. Two ounces of it contain only 143 calories. So if you're overweight and you have the money, you could conceivably go on an elegant diet of caviar.

TWENTY

A Big Caviar Habit

The man who has too much caviar uses it to
lubricate his wheels.

—RUSSIAN PROVERB

Some individuals have developed such a taste for caviar that their consumption of the delicacy gives them a special niche in every importer's heart.

And the fine restaurants of the world certainly wouldn't think of opening their doors without an adequate supply of the Caspian's black berries on hand.

One such restaurant was Le Pavillon of New York. Its proprietor, Henri Soulé, inherited the unofficial title of Baron of Caviar when its original holder, Ernest Byfield of the Ambassador Hotel in Chicago, passed away.

Legends about Henri Soulé abound. It's been said that he held a tiny gold ball on a chain over each tin of caviar. If the ball moved, the caviar was not first-rate.

When Malcolm Beyer was new to the caviar business, he visited Henri Soulé at Le Pavillon. Beyer brought five "pots" of fresh beluga with him

171

for Soulé to inspect and pass critical judgment on. At that time, a pot of caviar weighed about four pounds, and the going rate for a pot was approximately two hundred dollars.

Soulé opened each pot and spooned caviar from them. His expressive face indicated his displeasure until he sampled from the fifth pot. "Thees is for Soulé" he exclaimed.

Beyer left with the four opened and rejected pots. He had managed to satisfy New York's leading caviar demigod. Le Pavillon was a very prestigious account. "Besides," Beyer said, "even if it cost me money, I had to get started someplace."

But after months of departing from the restaurant with opened and unsalable tins of caviar because Soulé had rejected them, Beyer became angry. He knew, after all, that there simply wasn't much difference between one tin of fresh beluga and another. In some cases the sturgeon number on the tins was identical.

Once, just before Christmas, the busiest time for anyone in caviar, Beyer brought his samples to Soulé and watched as the master went through his tasting ritual. Finally, Soulé chose a tin and said, "Thees is for Soulé!"

At that point the tall, burly former marine general picked up an open, rejected pot of caviar, pushed it squarely into Soulé's face, and said, "No, *thees* is for Soulé!"

Soulé literally had egg on his face. He also proved himself a classy gentleman where Beyer was concerned, because he didn't take the account away; he remained a valued and lucrative customer.

General Beyer wasn't the only one who had to deal with difficult caviar buyers. I had my own moment of truth one afternoon with the chief of purchasing for a large international airline.

This gentleman arrived with two of his assistants at a special caviar tasting I'd set up for him. His airline served caviar on many of its flights and had been purchasing it from one of my competitors. I had persuaded him to give us a try, and I was confident that the caviar we had to offer would prove more pleasing to him once he tasted it.

What I didn't count on was that the buyer hated caviar. He couldn't bear to place a single sturgeon egg in his mouth. The expensive champagne and vodka I served at the tasting were also of no interest to him.

"I'd like a beer," he told me. "And a hamburger for lunch."

The buyer's assistants stood silently at his side, their mouths watering at the sight of superb beluga, osetra, and sevruga caviar tantalizingly displayed on an elegantly set table.

Caviar service at La Folie, New York. *Photo courtesy La Folie.*

Alfred Hitchcock with two
caviar-loving models.

"Go ahead, taste it," the buyer finally told the young men.

And they did, loving every mouthful.

When the buyer was ready to leave, I asked him whether we could discuss price.

"Sure," he replied. "Personally, I can't stand the stuff, but my assistants seemed to enjoy it."

We struck a price, and he became a customer even though I never did quite figure out how to sell caviar to a man who detests it.

Ernest Byfield was one of the nation's leading hotel men and restaurateurs. He ran the distinguished Ambassador and Sherman Hotels in Chicago, as well as their fine and famous restaurants, the Pump Room and Buttery at the Ambassador and the Well-of-the-Sea at the Sherman.

Byfield, like many other restaurateurs who serve caviar to their patrons, never made a profit from it. It was simply his own love for the elegant that prompted him to include beluga on the menu. Also, he personally loved caviar and often indulged in large quantities of it, washed down with the best Latvian vodka. (Legend has it that he died from going on an excessively stringent diet. He decided to diet when his corpulent belly would no longer slip behind the wheel of his Jaguar.)

The Pump Room in the Ambassador was one of few places where finely minced breast of pheasant could be ordered sprinkled over the beluga malossol. Being served by footmen in knee breeches from a specially designed rolling cart, on which a replica of St. Basil's Cathedral in Moscow housed the black sturgeon eggs, added to the panache of an evening in Byfield's establishment.

When the late Dave Chasen, whose Los Angeles restaurant bears his name, came to Iron Gate, he often waited until an hour before his airplane was due to depart New York for California. Then he would choose the tins of caviar he wanted and personally escort them home.

There are a number of people who see caviar as the perfect gift. I have customers who regularly come in and order tins of beluga malossol to be sent to friends all over the world. I have standing orders from certain customers to send a tin a month to a favorite friend, family member, or lover. One French gentleman arrives just before each Christmas and orders tins of our best beluga to be sent to a list of friends—one hundred of them. It's the only time we ever see him.

A good amount of caviar is ordered by the caterers whose reputations demand its inclusion on any party or dinner menu. Recently, at a birthday party for Studio 54, the now defunct New York disco, some fifty pounds of beluga was devoured by the celebrity guests. Ed Bonds, who catered what turned out to be a prime New York media event, had originally ordered thirty-five pounds, which were quickly eaten. A rush call and delivery replenished the caviar table.

Stories about big users of caviar are legion. I've had wealthy Latin Americans come to Iron Gate and buy ten and twenty kilos of caviar. They always pay with crisp one-hundred-dollar bills.

Heads of state send messengers for caviar.

Once, a man appeared and said he wanted to buy caviar for an unnamed government official. His order amounted to thirty-five hundred dollars' worth of the black berries. He handed me what I assumed were thirty-five one-hundred-dollar bills. I counted them while he stood there. There were thirty-six of them, and I handed one back to him.

"You're an honest man," he said. "I'll buy more from you."

And he has. He'd tested me, and I'd passed the test.

There's a Midwestern beer baron who has one pound of beluga shipped to him on the first of every month.

The wife of a distillery executive became a customer. She put in an order stating that her son could order all the caviar he wanted for one year. He placed orders for a few months, then became bored. We never heard from him again.

An exclusive Westchester, New York, country club has a monthly board of directors meeting. The meeting never begins until a pound of caviar has been served and consumed. Whether this ritual goes into the minutes is something I've not been privy to.

David Mishkin of Arizona is not the biggest fan of airline food. Before taking flights out of New York he picks up a half pound of caviar to eat on his trip.

The Sheriff's Panel Dinner in New York always begins with twenty-five pounds of caviar.

Recently, King Hussein of Jordan was to return to his native country after having conferred with President Carter in Washington, D.C. We were called on Monday and told that His Majesty wished to have ten pounds of beluga on the flight, which was to leave at noon the following day. One of my people took the shuttle to Washington, two thousand dollars' worth of caviar iced and carried on his lap in a thermo-bag.

The caviar delivered to King Hussein in Washington was all of the same type. Obviously, he's a democratic king—everyone in his party ate the same thing.

But when the queen of Saudi Arabia recently ordered caviar for her TWA charter flight back to Arabia, one pound of beluga malossol was for her. Ten pounds of sevruga was served to the rest of her entourage.

Salvador Dali is a confirmed caviar lover.

A wealthy patron of the arts once brought a three-pound container of caviar to Dali at his home in Spain.

Dali spooned large globs of it into his mouth. When his appetite was sated, he decided to be democratic. The artist covered the container and went from his house to the nearby beach where local fishermen were at work repairing their nets.

"Here," he said in his native Catalan, "I received a present, and I share it with you."

The fishermen, quite aware that their neighbor was the world's most famous living painter, were profuse in their thanks.

Dali left.

He returned to his house and went upstairs, where he could peek through the curtain. He watched the men pass the can from hand to hand. Each fisherman smelled it. Each made a face. Finally one lifted his arm and tossed the caviar into the ocean as far as he could throw.

The fishermen, never before having encountered caviar, thought the maestro had given them a can of spoiled fish.

A Peruvian hanger-on once approached Dali while the wax-moustached artist sat with his wife, Gala, at an open-air café.

Caviar served with crepes. *Photo: Marlies Jung.*

Blinis and caviar. *Photo: Marlies Jung.*

"Maestro, please take me to New York with you," the Peruvian pleaded. "I require very little. Just a little bread and butter and cheese."

Dali stood up indignantly. "Bread and butter and cheese! Caviar and champagne I am always given free by my admirers. But bread and butter and cheese? These cost money. Those I would have to order and pay for. No. No America! You stay here."

I have indicated earlier that caviar is a matter of personal taste. Dali's former manager, Captain J. Peter Moore, and his wife, Catherine, have three ocelots, two of which are named Babu and Bouba. The cats are rather famous in Europe. The couple rarely travels anywhere without at least Babu, who recently celebrated his eighteenth birthday.

Babu scorns caviar, but Bouba loves it. Whenever the Moores serve caviar—and it is often—Bouba is allowed to lick the empty container for what random few eggs still remain.

President John F. Kennedy was a devotee of caviar. He often served it at White House gatherings. Usually, we'd receive a call at Iron Gate from Mrs. Kennedy's secretary, Letitia Baldrige. The first time we received her call, she asked that the caviar she ordered be placed upon an afternoon train to Washington.

"I'm sorry," she was told, "but that wouldn't work."

"Of course it will," she replied. "There's a certain conductor on that train who will personally receive the caviar and see that it is delivered to the White House." She gave us the conductor's name and number. We contacted him and delivered to him the initial order for the White House.

Many pounds of the best caviar traveled between New York and Washington on that train, in the hands of that special conductor.

Obviously, we enjoyed having the president and the first lady as customers.

On December 12, 1909, the Romanoff Caviar Company, then known as the Russian Caviar Company, received the following letter.

The Russian Caviar Company
115 Reade Street
New York, N.Y.

Dear Sirs:

Please send me one large box holding three pounds, three ounces of caviar. It is to be used for dinner Thursday night.

Very truly,

H. H. Taft (Mrs. W. H. Taft)

It was on White House stationery.

Speaking of first ladies, we've always had heavy and consistent customers among the rich Greek tycoons of shipping and oil. One such international mogul often orders as much as thirty pounds of our best available product to give away as gifts. It isn't unusual for him to buy six or seven thousand dollars' worth of beluga malossol and pressed caviar at a time. We're very quick to service him. His checks are always as sound as his palate.

The holiday season is the busiest time of the year for every caviar merchant. During the 1978 Christmas season, the famous Macy's Cellar of New York called us on Friday at 5:00 P.M. New Year's Eve was on Sunday.

Macy's had run an impressive ad for its caviar, and the impact of the ad had evidently been substantial. The cupboard was just about bare.

"Can you deliver some caviar to us right now?" I was asked.

I said I assumed we could. Even though our supplies were low, we had enough in storage to service a modest request. "How much do you want?" I asked.

"Forty-five pounds."

A sterling-silver sturgeon service for caviar. *Photo: Marlies Jung.*

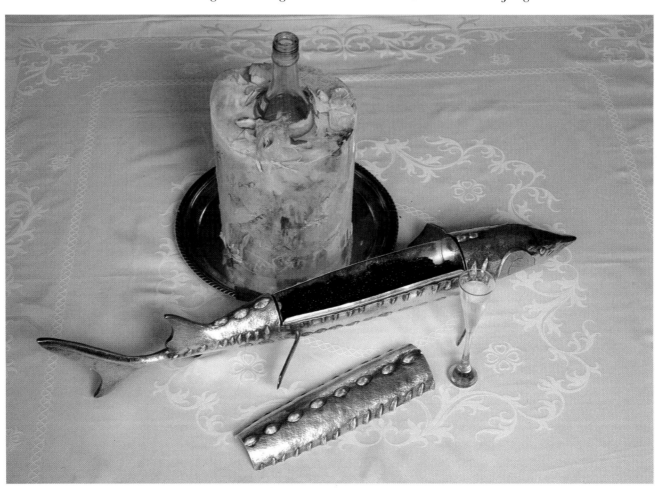

I composed myself, made a few mental calculations, and agreed that we would deliver within two hours. We kept our promise. I managed to catch a few of our employees as they were getting ready to go home, persuaded them to stay and prepare the Macy's order, and personally delivered it to the store in my automobile (which bears the license plate CAVIAR 1). The transaction represented almost ten thousand dollars' worth of last-minute business.

A similar situation occurred at the holiday season with a Las Vegas hotel. This rush order was for fifty pounds of our best caviar. It was on a jet airplane within hours.

One of my personal favorite customers is the food editor of the *New York Times,* Mimi Sheraton.

About two years ago I received a call from Ms. Sheraton requesting an interview for a piece she intended to write on caviar for the *Times.* Actually, the article devoted itself primarily to pressed caviar, which, I was later to learn, was her favorite.

During the interview, I was impressed with the immense knowledge she already possessed about caviar. I told her what I could and hoped I'd been of help. I also hoped what she wrote would be favorable to me, to my company, and to the product we sell.

I needn't have worried. Up until the time the article appeared in the *Times,* we would sell a moderate amount of pressed caviar each month. The pressed variety is much more popular with Europeans than it is with Americans.

Within three days after the article appeared, we sold almost four hundred pounds of pressed caviar, much more than we'd sold during the past six months. The power of the press at work. I suppose what had happened was that many lovers of fresh, whole caviar were prompted to try the pressed type. After all, if it was good enough for the food editor of the *New York Times,* it was good enough for them.

Ms. Sheraton has become a valued personal customer. Each year she comes to our warehouse around the holiday period and personally chooses and picks up her beloved pressed caviar. Last year, however, as I noted earlier, she also purchased some osetra. It was just too good for her to pass up.

I've been interviewed many times, but one of the most pleasant experiences I can remember involved the legendary and creative merchant Stanley Marcus, founder of Neiman-Marcus of Dallas. Mr. Marcus is a man of great taste and refinement. His love of everything elegant is well-known, and he was prompted to write a book on the elegant things in life. Happily, he chose to include a chapter on caviar.

When Mr. Marcus called me and requested an interview, I readily accepted the opportunity. I suggested we meet at the 21 Club, and we introduced ourselves to each other at three one sunny afternoon.

Because I was anxious to impress Mr. Marcus favorably with the quality of caviar handled by my firm, I decided to bring to the interview three four-ounce tins of our best, one of beluga, one of osetra, and one of sevruga.

When Mr. Marcus realized that it was my intention to open the tins and to invite him to feast on their contents, he became quite animated. We talked at length about caviar, and I trust I was helpful to him by sharing my knowledge. However, I would never be so naïve as to ignore the potency of those tins of the best caviar available in New York. Not only did Stanley Marcus *hear* about caviar, but his taste buds experienced what the words were saying. It was an afternoon I shall always treasure.

Show-business and literary people have always had a particular love for the taste of black berries. The late novelist Jacqueline Susann often dipped into a tin of beluga for breakfast. The immense sales of her novels allowed her this gourmet indulgence.

In the Broadway hit *Noël Coward in Two Keys,* Anne Baxter got to eat caviar on stage each night because it was written into the script.

And Anthony Quayle enjoyed caviar on stage during each performance of *Sleuth.* His script was even better than Ms. Baxter's, however. Quayle washed his caviar down during each performance with a glass of champagne.

TWENTY-ONE

In Praise of Romance Once Again

To conclude.

What is caviar?

Sturgeon eggs?

If you prefer to view it in such a pedantic manner.

But just as a jet airplane is the sum and substance of millions of parts and wires and switches and dials, it is ultimately a very romantic magic carpet upon which to fly away to exotic places.

To a carpenter, a house consists of joists, foundations, gutters, and concrete. To those who share love and warmth within the house, it is something else entirely.

And so it is with caviar. To eat it, to serve it, is to indulge in romance. And what finer way to spend one's life than to conduct a love affair with life itself?

For valentine's day we will have a special menu and a special evening. For a wonderful surprise and an out of the ordinary treat, bring your loved one to Arisbtt. they will never forget it.

Caviar service on Trans World Airlines. *Photo courtesy Trans World Airlines, Inc.*

TWENTY-TWO

The Ayatollah and Me

Ayatollah who?

Until January 1979, few people in the western world knew or cared about a bearded Iranian Muslim leader known as Ayatollah Ruhollah Khomeini. I certainly count myself in that group. When it came to Iranian caviar, the only person who had my undivided attention was Shah Mohammed Riza Pahlevi, Iran's royal dictator who saw to it that caviar, and Iran's other precious black commodity, oil, got sold to the rest of the world with regularity, at a handsome profit for Iran and the royal family.

But in January 1979, the shah was asked to leave Iran by zealous followers of Ayatollah Khomeini, and the world will never be the same, politically or gastronomically.

Here's what happened.

Under the shah, the Iranian caviar industry was administered with an iron hand. Fishermen went out each day, hauled in their sturgeon, and turned everything over to government representatives of the Iranian *shilot* through which all caviar was marketed. The fishermen were paid little for their efforts, even though one five-hundred-pound sturgeon with fifty pounds of caviar in its belly could be worth five thousand dollars. Naturally, there was a temptation on the fishermen's part to hold back a few berries for the black market, but they seldom did. It wasn't worth the punishment. Embezzling caviar in the shah's Iran was as serious an offense as scribbling graffiti about the shah's wife on an Iranian men's-room wall.

For the caviar-consuming world, Iran's neat and tidy caviar industry under the shah meant a relatively steady supply of good-grade caviar at high, albeit stable prices.

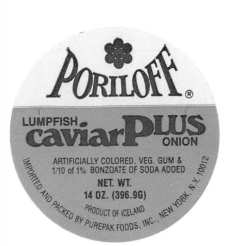

Then, January 1979. The ayatollah decreed that Iran would return to a strict Muslim state, which meant no music, dancing, drinking, whoring, or drug dealing, It also meant *no caviar,* not for consumption *or* for sale. But then commercial realism prevailed and the dictates set down by regional *mullahs* were amended to allow caviar to be sold outside the country. No sense in being too strict in interpreting the Koran. The government *shilot* remained in business, and the fishermen were again expected to turn over their daily catch to the ayatollah's representatives.

But changes brought about by the shift in government were too sweeping to be ignored. The country was in chaos, and the shah's iron fist was in evidence no longer. The new government passed many new laws, but the enforcement capability simply wasn't there. More important, the citizens, including the Iranian fishermen, knew it. They realized that now was the time to improve their slice of the caviar pie. Why turn it all over to the ayatollah's inefficient *shilot?* All they had to do was to figure out a way to market their catch to Europe, the United States, and the rest of the world.

But then an old Islamic proverb reared its ugly head: "Easier said than done." The fishermen knew how to catch the fish, extract the roe, and package it for export but hadn't the foggiest notion how to get it out of the country and deliver it to big caviar buyers in exchange for cash on the barrelhead.

Enter one enterprising young Iranian whom I shall call Mohammed. To use his real name would be to ensure his death in Iran.

Mohammed was twenty-three years old. His family evidently had enough clout with the new government to allow him unrestricted travel in and out of the country. He was sort of a Muslim Sammy Glick, bright, ambitious, and always looking for a lucrative void into which he could leap. He found it with the Iranian sturgeon fishermen. His proposition to them was simple. He would pay them ten times more for their caviar than the government *shilot* had paid even in its most generous moments. He'd pay them in cash, no questions asked.

Pretty soon, Mohammed was up to his black curls in caviar, and it was time to put phase two of his plan into action.

I was sitting in my office at Iron Gate one afternoon in early May 1979, when a business associate called from Paris. After some initial chitchat, he said, "Gerry, you've got to come to Europe right away."

"Why?" I asked.

"There's a new source of Iranian caviar about to break that can deliver not only top quality, but can deliver it significantly cheaper than what the *shilot* is offering."

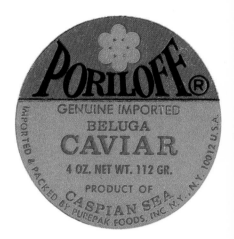

My friend answered my questions in vague terms. He really didn't know very much, he told me, and I believed him. Had he not been someone with whom I'd been dealing for many years, I might have dismissed his suggestion that I fly to Europe. But I had faith in his judgment, and what he'd told me was too provocative to ignore. Besides, I have never considered trips to Europe to be either a hardship or distasteful. I agreed to meet him in Paris later that week.

As I crossed the Atlantic, I became increasingly excited about why I was going. Since the shah had been deposed, the world caviar market had been in a state of flux. The ayatollah's new government had broken its caviar contract with Panacaviar's George Fixen. He'd sued Iran over the broken contract. Iran had then sued him in retaliation. Because Panacaviar supplied the Western Hemisphere with all its Iranian caviar, we were left with uncertain supplies, having to depend entirely upon the Soviet Union. If my friend in Paris was right, an important new source of caviar would be available to fill the gap.

There was another factor, however, that heightened my anticipation. Recently, some European caviar dealers had begun to sell at prices below what I could match—or even understand. At first, I'd wondered whether they were drawing from a three-ton batch that had been reported floating around Europe and, according to my sources, had been out of Iranian refrigeration too long. In a word, it was rapidly spoiling. Our own Food and Drug Administration had been informed of this tainted supply and had issued a worldwide alert.

But further research indicated that what was being sold below prevailing market prices was, in fact, of good quality. It was possible, I reasoned, that it was being drawn from the same supplier that my friend had told me about. If so, I wanted to be the first American to tap into this supply.

Caviar service on Pan
American World Airways.
*Photo courtesy Pan American
World Airways.*

I checked into my Paris hotel, then met my friend for dinner. He had little to add to his original story, but he did assure me that after dinner we would receive all the information we needed from the proverbial horse's mouth, the new and mysterious Iranian supplier.

Mohammed came to the hotel later that evening, and my friend introduced me to him. Frankly, my initial impression was that I'd been the victim of an expensive joke. Mohammed wore blue jeans, white sneakers, and a Walt Disney T-shirt.

"*You're* offering me caviar?" I asked, unable to disguise my incredulity.

"Yes," he said.

"How much can you provide?"

"Tons."

"Tons?"

"All you want."

As we talked, I again thought of the tainted shipment that was reported to be in Europe, and I wondered whether I was being offered caviar of inferior quality. I asked Mohammed about this, and he replied that what he had to sell was the best Iran could offer, top-quality beluga, osetra, and sevruga.

"I'll have to see for myself," I said. "Where is it?"

Mohammed smiled. "In Iran, of course, but it is on its way."

"To Paris?"

He shook his head. "Denmark. Copenhagen."

I felt a little better about things now. When I'd held the Russian contract back in the sixties, I had moved every ounce of Soviet caviar through Copenhagen. It's an excellent free port, with a smooth, efficient, and trouble-free system of customs. I personally knew many of the top Danish expediters and held them in the highest regard.

The three of us got on a plane the next day and flew to Copenhagen. For some reason I expected to at least be shown samples of what Mohammed had to offer. I expected too much. He had nothing there, not even one tin of the caviar he was trying to sell.

I angrily asked, "Why did you bring me all the way to Europe if you don't have anything to show me?"

"To make sure you were serious," Mohammed said, still smiling. "Now that I know you are, the caviar will come."

I made it plain to him that I would not buy sight unseen and that I would personally insist upon inspecting every tin being offered. He balked and suggested that I sample only representative tins from whole lots. Under ordinary circumstances, that would have sufficed. In all my years of dealing with the Russians, and with the Iranians under the shah, I'd never had a problem with the quality of caviar delivered by them. The processing and packing operations in both countries had always been accomplished under strict supervision, and quality control had been exemplary.

But this was different. I was like an addict about to buy from an unknown street source. Worse, I would be left with no legal recourse should the product not live up to its promised standards.

We debated for an hour. Finally, Mohammed agreed that I could personally taste and inspect each tin he brought in to Copenhagen. Our deal was that I would pay him for each tin I accepted, but only after I had approved it. I flew to New York to await a call telling me that the shipment had arrived.

That call came shortly before Memorial Day weekend. I returned to Copenhagen, this time with an extra suitcase containing my own jeans, sweat shirts, and rubber boots. I also had with me commitments from two other major U.S. caviar merchants. The heads of those companies had authorized me to buy for them, too, which was flattering.

After checking into the Plaza Hotel (I was to end up spending so much time there that they eventually gave me a handsome discount), I changed into my work clothes and headed for the Danish fish market, where the on-site inspection would take place. Sure enough, Mohammed was there along with four big, burly associates, three of them Turkish and an Iranian. The tins of caviar were there too, waiting to be opened and their contents sampled.

I'd arranged through my Danish friends to have a crew of helpers available to me. As it turned out, my crew consisted of six absolutely beautiful Danish females, each of whom held another job but had agreed to moonlight. It provided quite a contrast, four swarthy, husky men on one side of long tables that had been set up for my use, six blond beauties on the other side, and me in the middle. I felt like El Exigente.

The first green tin was set before me. I carefully opened it. Usually, tins of caviar are secured with thick rubber bands, but the ayatollah's government had evidently banned rubber bands, because strips of inner tubes had been pressed into service. I visually inspected the sturgeon roe in the can, sniffed it, then raised a tiny portion to my mouth.

It was incredibly good. I smiled and nodded. Mohammed grinned and looked at his helpers. The Danes simply stood there, their faces void of emotion.

After inspecting a few more tins, I realized that none of the caviar had been graded into the usual categories of beluga, osetra, or sevruga. I asked Mohammed about this and he said, "There was no time."

"I'll have to grade them then," I said.

"Why?"

"Because that's the way it's done. Beluga is worth more than sevruga."

Mohammed looked at his asociates, none of whom appeared to be in sympathy with my needs. He then said, "We will grade it."

I shook my head. "We had a deal," I reminded him. "I make all the determinations, and that includes grading."

A pause, then a vehement shaking of his head. "This is not fair," he said.

I shrugged and said, "It doesn't matter. Either we do it my way or I take my money and go home."

That seemed to do it. He reluctantly agreed, and the inspection continued.

After years in the caviar trade, I'd learned to temper any overt enthusiasm in front of a seller. All that accomplishes is to prompt the seller to raise his price. That's why I restrained myself on the docks of Copenhagen. The fact was, however, that Mohammed had delivered caviar as fine as I'd seen in years. There were even tins of golden osetra that hadn't been seen by anyone for years, with the exception of Russian and Iranian rulers.

I was giddy with my find and worked feverishly to inspect and categorize as many tins as possible before the day ended. My Danish helpers were efficient and pleasant, and the assembly line I'd created was soon rolling along in full gear. After smelling and tasting the contents of each tin, I handed the tin to one of the women, who carefully trimmed and cleaned it. She, in turn, handed it to another woman for weighing on a computer scale to determine its exact weight. Then it went into a foam container packed with dry ice, six tins to a container. Originally, I'd planned to vacuum seal each container in a shrink bag, but our first attempt at this resulted in the explosion of one of the tins. We settled for drawing as much air as possible out of the bags.

By the end of the first day I was exhausted—and delighted. I returned to the Plaza, where I showered, shaved, changed into a suit, and joined my Middle Eastern and Danish friends for dinner. The mood was ebullient and the liquor flowed freely. Mohammed drank despite his Muslim upbringing. His associates did not, preferring orange juice

Caviar service on Pan Am. *Photo courtesy Pan American World Airways.*

or water. I admired them for that. They were far from home, yet adhered to their beliefs.

The inspection of Mohammed's caviar went on for another four days. There were a few disappointments. Some of the best caviar had to be tossed in a garbage pail because it had been too lightly salted and had begun to turn. The fishermen and processors back in Iran hadn't adjusted yet to the fact that the best of the catch would not be going to Iranian royalty for quick consumption, as had usually been the case in the past. The one or two percent salt they'd added to the golden osetra hadn't been enough to preserve it during the long trek to Copenhagen. I could have cried as I tossed tins of it away. Had it been treated with four and a half or five percent salt, it would have survived perfectly.

One of the things that amazed me throughout those five days on the docks of Copenhagen was the network Mohammed had created to spirit his supplies out of Iran. Because all caviar was supposed to go through the government *shilot,* Mohammed was engaged in smuggling on a grand scale. He'd established a remarkable cabal that used suitcases, steamer trunks, canvas bags, anything to transport Iran's other "black gold" to Denmark. Iranian trucks that routinely made runs through Turkey into Europe were being used. I can only assume that Mohammed had paid off the drivers of those trucks. He wouldn't discuss the details of his system with me, and I couldn't blame him. Besides, I really didn't care. The bottom line was that he'd delivered what he'd promised, and that was good news for me and for the world's caviar lovers.

I left Copenhagen the proud owner of more than four hundred kilograms of assorted top-quality Iranian caviar. I'd given Mohammed more than a hundred thousand dollars, and I promised to return once this initial shipment cleared U.S. Customs and our FDA. There was still a question about that in my mind. Although Mohammed had assured me that only pure salt had been used, there was always the possibility that some borax had been added. If it had, tests run in America would pick it up, and the shipment would be denied entry. As it turned out, the shipment breezed through U.S. Customs. We were home free, and my associates joined me for a celebratory bottle of champagne.

I returned to Copenhagen over Labor Day weekend. This time, Mohammed had pulled out all the stops. Caviar poured into Denmark in its familiar green and blue tins. Mohammed's cadre of couriers had grown and now included passengers on commercial airliners who filled their suitcases with tins. A boat arrived laden with Iranian caviar, and private automobiles hauled in boxes filled with tins.

Other things had changed too. The weather had turned sharply colder; I wore long johns beneath my jeans and added thermal socks to my boots.

Mohammed wasn't dressed the same, either. Walt Disney had been replaced by Gucci—Gucci loafers and an ornate belt buckle. He wore an expensive three-piece suit, a white silk shirt open at the neck, and strands of gold chain around his neck. He'd taken the finest suite of rooms in the best hotels and was now accompanied, in addition to his male helpers, by a stunning young woman who was introduced to me as his wife. I learned later that it was a common-law marriage and that she had provided much of the brainpower behind his ambitious scheme.

We worked the usual ten-hour days in frigid conditions, and we had little energy left at night to enjoy Copenhagen's myriad of delights.

The caviar that resulted from this second trip to Copenhagen had a significant impact upon the American market at Christmas, the busiest time of year for all caviar merchants. Because Mohammed's prices were significantly lower than what the Iranian *shilot* was offering, we were able to lower our consumer prices, a remarkable feat in the face of raging inflation and a caviar market that had done nothing but show increased prices over the years.

The following October, I was contacted by European caviar brokers who asked me to arrange an introduction to this new and wonderful source of quality Iranian caviar. I agreed and met them in Copenhagen in early November. By now, the Danish weather was frigid. Their order was relatively small, and when I'd completed the inspection ritual on their behalf, I turned to a new batch to supplement my own Christmas supply. The quality of Mohammed's latest delivery was as good as that of previous deliveries, and I remember thinking to myself as the day progressed that I really should send a telegram of appreciation to the ayatollah for making all this possible. It was a whimsical thought that disappeared as quickly as it had been conceived.

I was about to call it a day, when a Danish official handed me a telegram. I removed the rubber gloves I wore, opened the envelope, and read the telegram. The message was short and to the point. The American embassy in Tehran had been seized by young revolutionaries, and embassy employees were being held hostage. It was November 4, 1979.

I went to the Plaza, had a quiet dinner, and contemplated what this unlikely event in Iran would mean to the world and, more narrowly, to the American attitude toward Iranian products. Waiting at Copenhagen's airport to be shipped to the United States was almost a half million dollars' worth of Iranian caviar. It had been paid for, inspected, repack-

aged, and stored for shipment. Would Americans react strongly
enough to the embassy takeover to decide not to buy anything Iranian?
I doubted it. After all, no one kept hostages very long, did they? I assumed that a few days would pass, the hostages would be released, and
the entire incident would be forgotten. Still, I wanted to confer with
others back in New York before authorizing the shipment. The confer-
ence, which took place a few days later, resulted in a decision to bring in
all the caviar we could from Copenhagen.

We did it in two shipments, the second arriving just one day before
America's dockworkers, as well as hotel and restaurant unions, decided
not to handle Iranian goods.

We had more meetings about the situation and decided that even
though the hostage crisis seemed to be dragging on and perhaps would
for some time, the Russians had an ample supply of caviar to draw
upon. However, that cushion threatened to crumble in December,
when the Soviet Union invaded Afghanistan. For those of us in the
caviar business, there suddenly loomed the distinct possibility that
Americans would boycott anything grown, fished, or manufactured in
Iran and the Soviet Union. Since those two nations were the only two
games in town where caviar was concerned, you can understand why we
were less than optimistic about the future.

In January, there was a strong tide of sentiment in the United States
for a general boycott of all Iranian goods. Even without such a boycott,
I'd decided to forgo bringing in any more Iranian caviar until the hostage question had been resolved. I informed Mohammed of my decision, and he reacted angrily. "The hostages will be released," he told
me. "I have friends in high places in Tehran, and they assure me that it
will soon be over."

I wasn't satisfied with his assurances and told him so. His response
was all business. He told me that if I didn't continue to deal with him
throughout the hostage crisis, when it was over I could go back to buying from the government *shilot.*

He meant it. Everyone in the worldwide caviar trade knew about Mohammed by this time and was anxious to get a piece of his action. Because I'd been first, I had the inside position, and I hated to lose it. I
told him I'd get back to him in a few days, then started calling potential
brokers in the Far East, South America, and Europe. I lined up an
impressive list of buyers and flew off to Copenhagen with their orders
tucked in my briefcase. Mohammed seemed appreciative of my efforts,
and he told me that whenever I felt it was appropriate to bring his

product into the United States again, he would be ready to deliver to me, and only to me.

I took delivery of my last batch of Mohammed's Iranian caviar on January 22, 1980. It had been contracted for early in the hostage crisis and would be the last I would see from my young Iranian's supply. The American boycott against Iran was imposed, and it was complete. From that day forward, all caviar brought into the United States through me and my company, Iron Gate, has been Russian. Naturally, the prices have gone up again and are back to what they were pre-Mohammed.

I suppose Mohammed continued to sell to other countries and through other wholesalers. But my international sources tell me that he seemed to fade from the caviar marketplace. We could only speculate that he either was removed from the market by the ayatollah's government during a trip back home or found a new and more lucrative market, the Soviet Union. It's easy for one nation to sell to another and to have that second nation package the product under its own flag to avoid high government tariffs or political restrictions. I've recently been trying to trace down the source of caviar being packaged under a Yugoslavian label. To my knowledge, there are no sturgeon in Yugoslavia. It is, however, considered a developing nation and, therefore, is exempt from paying duty. Whether another country with sturgeon is using Yugoslavia as an outlet for caviar remains to be seen.

Some of the domestic pressure caused by the American boycott against Iranian caviar has been eased by our own emerging caviar industry. Since I started work on this book, there has been a dramatic increase in the supply and quality of American sturgeon. I recently had the pleasure of supplying all the caviar for one of President Reagan's Pre-inaugural cocktail parties, and every ounce of it was American. I expect to handle between twelve and thirteen tons of it in 1981 and even more in the future. Samples have been sent to Europe's finest restaurants, including Maxim's of Paris, and to the world's leading airlines and steamship companies. It's good caviar and, because it's home-grown, costs considerably less than its Iranian and Russian competition. And by the way, I'm not talking about American lumpfish and whitefish eggs, dyed black to look like the real thing. I'm talking about American sturgeon roe taken from the rivers of California, Oregon, and Tennessee and New York's Hudson.

Since the American boycott against Iranian goods, a whole new group of "Mohammeds" have sprung up. They wander into my offices off the street and tell me about a "cousin" through whom they can get me the best Iranian caviar. I've sat through lunches in executive dining rooms with Iranian businessmen who tell me the same thing. Lately, there always seems to be an invitation to a party at which I'll be introduced to "Mr. Caviar," a close friend of the ayatollah who'll choke my warehouses with Iranian caviar at bargain-basement prices.

Just as I was finishing this chapter, I received a call from my friend in Paris who'd started the whole thing in May 1979. After exchanging pleasantries, he said he had someone in his office who wished to speak to me.

"Hello?" I said.

"Hello, Mr. Stein," said a voice. It was Mohammed. During our brief conversation he assured me of three things—he was still alive, he was still in business, and when the boycott against his country was lifted, I could count on him for caviar.

It was good talking to him. As a businessman, I'm glad he'll still be around to do business with. But more than that, I was relieved to hear his voice and to know that the ayatollah hadn't caught up with him. I grew to like Mohammed, and I look forward to seeing him again one day in Copenhagen.

Recipes

MY FAVORITES

Sunday Brunch

Occasionally, on a lazy Sunday morning in my home, my wife prepares what I consider the ultimate in sensuous, sinful sandwiches. And in all likelihood, they're the most expensive.

She toasts a Thomas' English muffin. A layer of caviar, either whole-grain or pressed, is liberally applied to one half of the muffin. Then she adds a slice of smoked salmon and a slice of sturgeon.

She places the other half of the muffin on top, and we're in for a Sunday brunch of extraordinary pleasure.

Another variation of this is to use cream cheese in place of the salmon and sturgeon.

Blinis

The ideal way to enjoy good caviar is to eat it plain.

But the exquisite taste of caviar adds dimension to so many other foods.

Blinis, those wonderful thin buckwheat pancakes, have always been a favorite companion to caviar.

Try smearing blinis with warm, melted sweet butter and wrapping them around a tablespoon of whole-grain caviar.

Or spread blinis with pressed caviar, then add some sour cream, and you have a dish that not only tastes wonderful, but looks attractive too.

(And don't forget plain old white bread if you're out of blinis and English muffins. Sweet butter spread on a slice of bread and garnished with caviar turns plebeian bread into an aristocratic delight.)

Making Your Own Blinis

Making your own blinis is easy and gives you the added pleasure of knowing that the caviar you spread on them or roll in them is going on the freshest and best.

There are basically two types of blinis, buckwheat and white flour.

In Macy's Cellar, Gregory ladles out the batter . . .

. . . flips the blinis when ready . . .

BUCKWHEAT BLINIS

1	cup milk
½	tablespoon yeast (about a half a package)
4	eggs, separated
½	teaspoon salt
1	teaspoon sugar
3	tablespoons melted butter
1½	cups sifted buckwheat flour

Put the milk in a saucepan and scald it. Allow to cool until lukewarm. Add the yeast and stir until softened. Beat the egg yolks until thickened. Add the yeast mixture to the remaining ingredients (except the egg whites). Mix thoroughly. Beat the egg whites until stiff. Fold gently into the batter. Lightly butter a griddle and preheat. Use one tablespoon of batter for each pancake. Bake on the griddle until golden brown, turning once. If the blinis begin to stick to the griddle, butter lightly again. Makes approximately thirty-six blinis.

WHITE-FLOUR BLINIS

2	cups milk
½	tablespoon yeast (about half a package)
3	cups sifted flour

2   teaspoons sugar
5   tablespoons melted butter
½   teaspoon salt
3   eggs, separated

Put the milk in a saucepan and scald it. Allow it to cool until lukewarm. Add the yeast and stir until it has softened. Add 1½ cups of flour and the sugar and mix thoroughly. Cover and allow to set in a pan of warm water until it has approximately doubled in bulk (about one and a half hours). Beat the butter and salt in with the egg yolks. Add to the batter. Add the remaining flour and beat until very smooth. Cover and allow it to rise, just as before, until the bulk doubles in size (approximately thirty minutes). Beat egg whites until stiff and fold them into the batter. Let the mixture stand for fifteen minutes. Preheat a lightly buttered griddle until hot. Spoon out one tablespoon of batter for each blini. Bake until golden brown on both sides, turning once. Makes approximately forty blinis.

(If you're in a rush, Aunt Jemima or any ready-to-make mix does very nicely too.)

. . . spoons on some sour cream . . .

. . . and adds the caviar. . . .

Then the author serves the first blini to George Kinzler.

Blinis with caviar. *Photo: Marlies Jung.*

CAVIAR WITH DEVILED EGGS

Deviled eggs are a staple on any appetizer table. Shell five hardboiled eggs. Cut them in half lengthwise and remove the yolks. After mashing the yolks to the consistency of fine paste, add 2 teaspoons of lemon juice and 2 tablespoons of mayonnaise. (Sour cream does nicely too.) Add a little salt and pepper to taste. Replace the mashed yolks in the hollows of the egg whites but leave a shallow indentation in the yolks. Add a tiny amount (about 1/5 teaspoon) of whole-grain caviar to each egg. This will give you ten deviled-egg-with-caviar appetizers.

OPEN STEAK SANDWICHES AND CAVIAR

The open steak sandwich has always been a favorite, particularly as a late-night supper treat. But the steak sandwich can be lifted to new heights by using caviar as a visually appealing and tasty garnish.

1   15-ounce loaf of French bread
    Sweet, unsalted butter
1   1-pound piece tender steak (filet, sirloin, or rib), cooked
4   tablespoons whole-grain caviar
1   bunch green onions

Split the French bread vertically. Cut two slices from the center, each about ½ inch thick. Broil the two slices to a toasty brown, then butter them. Slice the cold steak (the thinner the slices the better; be sure to have trimmed off all fat first). Divide the slices of steak evenly and place half of them on each piece of toasted bread. Salt lightly. Spoon a strip of caviar down the center of each sandwich. Use 2 tablespoons for each. Garnish with a few green onion tops and place the remaining green onions around the slices, on a serving tray. Cut in sections and serve. Makes about eight servings.

Shrimp on toast with caviar. *Photo: Marlies Jung.*

SHRIMP ON TOAST WITH CAVIAR

This makes a pretty and tasty appetizer.

white Melba toast
30 to 40 shelled, deveined medium shrimp
sour cream
black whole-grain caviar
lemon wedges (optional)

Place one shrimp on each slice of Melba toast. Spoon about ½ teaspoon sour cream into the curve of each shrimp. Spoon ½ teaspoon of caviar onto top of sour cream. Serve with lemon wedge to be squeezed over the appetizer (optional).

CAVIAR MOUSSE

2   tablespoons cold water
1   tablespoon unflavored gelatin
½   cup boiling water
2   tablespoons lemon juice
2   tablespoons mayonnaise

hot sauce
½   cup (about 4 ounces) caviar
2   cups sour cream
lettuce leaves

Soften the gelatin in the cold water. Add ½ cup boiling water and stir until the gelatin is completely dissolved. Allow to cool slightly. Mix in the lemon juice and the mayonnaise. Add the hot sauce and stir. Add the caviar and the sour cream and stir to a creamy blend. Pour into a shallow dish and chill until fully set. Cut into squares and serve on lettuce leaves, either as an appetizer or as hors d'oeuvres. Makes six to eight servings.

Oysters with caviar. *Photo: Marlies Jung.*

Open steak sandwich with caviar. *Photo: Marlies Jung.*

CAVIAR SANDWICHES WITH LIVERWURST AND ONIONS

Pumpernickel bread (Westphalian style)
Thin slices of mild onion
Thin slices of liverwurst or Braunschweiger
Sour cream
Black, whole-grain caviar (3 tablespoons for every six sandwiches)
Minced mild onion (2 tablespoons for every six sandwiches)

Place one slice of onion and two slices of liverwurst on each slice of pumpernickel. Spoon three teaspoons of sour cream into the middle of each open sandwich. Mix the caviar and minced onion and place a small amount on the sour cream.

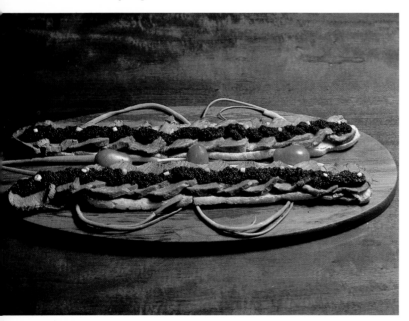

LOW-CALORIE RECIPES

CAVIAR YOGURT DIP

⅔   cup plain yogurt
2   ounces caviar
1   tablespoon minced parsley
2   teaspoons grated onion and juice
1   teaspoon prepared mustard

Combine all ingredients. Serve at once or cover and chill. Just before serving, stir. Good with unsalted crackers or crisp raw vegetables. Makes about 1 cup, enough for six to eight.

CAVIAR DEVILED EGGS

12 eggs, hard-boiled and shelled
6 tablespoons regular or low-calorie mayonnaise
1 teaspoon prepared spicy mustard
¼ teaspoon Tabasco
2 tablespoons (1 ounce) caviar
   Additional caviar for garnish

Cut eggs in half, lengthwise. With tip of spoon, remove yolk. Mash with mayonnaise, mustard, and Tabasco. Fold in caviar. Spoon into whites. Garnish with additional caviar. Makes twenty-four halves.

CAVIAR-STUFFED TOMATOES

6 medium tomatoes
2 cups cottage cheese
2 tablespoons chopped chives
¼ cup grated carrot
   dash black pepper
4 tablespoons caviar
   lettuce and lemon wedges for garnish

Cut a thin horizontal slice from the top of each tomato. Remove seeds and some of pulp; set aside, turned upside-down on paper toweling to drain. Combine cottage cheese, chives, carrot, and pepper. Chill about one hour. At serving time, turn tomatoes right-side up, fill with cottage cheese mixture, and top each with a spoonful of caviar. Set on lettuce-lined plate and garnish with lemon wedge. Makes six servings.

CAVIAR POTATO SALAD

10 medium potatoes, peeled and thinly sliced (6 cups)
6 tablespoons oil
3 tablespoons vinegar
3 tablespoons lemon juice
¼ cup of chopped onion

Platter of caviar hors d'oeuvres. *Photo: Marlies Jung.*

English muffins with caviar, sturgeon, and salmon, served with tea and orange juice. *Photo: Marlies Jung.*

¼ teaspoon powdered dill
   dash salt and pepper
4 hard-boiled eggs, chopped
¼ cup mayonnaise
3 tablespoons caviar
   additional caviar for garnish

An elegant breakfast: English muffins and caviar, served with smoked salmon and sturgeon. *Photo: Marlies Jung.*

Cook potatoes in boiling salted water until barely tender, about eight minutes. Drain. In large bowl, combine oil, vinegar, lemon juice, onion, dill, salt, and pepper. Add potatoes; toss to coat. Mash eggs with mayonnaise. Gently stir in caviar and fold into potatoes. Cover; keep cold. At serving time, garnish with additional caviar. Makes eight generous servings.

1   can (about 7 ounces) salmon, drained and flaked
½   cup minced celery
1   tablespoon minced onion
¼   cup mayonnaise
2   tablespoons caviar
8   slices buttered pumpernickel

Combine salmon, celery, and onion. Add mayonnaise and caviar and blend gently. Spread on pumpernickel to make sandwiches. Enough for four.

MACARONI SALAD SUPREME

4   cups cooked elbow macaroni, drained and rinsed
½   cup each chopped celery and green pepper
¼   cup each finely chopped scallions and parsley

3   tablespoons wine vinegar
¾   cup mayonnaise
4   tablespoons caviar
    crisp salad greens

Combine macaroni with vegetables. Stir vinegar into mayonnaise along with caviar. Add to macaroni; mix well. Chill. Serve on salad greens. Makes eight servings.

CHILLED SHRIMP WITH CAVIAR DRESSING

1   pound medium or jumbo fresh or frozen shrimp
1   cup mayonnaise
2   tablespoons caviar

1   tablespoon well-drained horseradish
1   teaspoon lemon juice
    lettuce leaves

If necessary, thaw and shell shrimp. Cook, following package directions if frozen. (Drop fresh shrimp in boiling salted water and boil uncovered only until pink.) Drain and chill well. Combine mayonnaise, caviar, horseradish, and lemon juice in serving bowl. Arrange shrimp on bed of lettuce and serve with hors d'oeuvre picks and dip. Enough for six.

SIDE DISHES AND SALADS

CAVIAR VEGETABLE BOWL

2   cucumbers, peeled
2   tomatoes, peeled
2   carrots, pared
¼   cup grated sweet onion and juice
3   ounces cream cheese, softened

1   cup sour cream
¼   cup mayonnaise
1   tablespoon lemon juice
4   tablespoons caviar
    lettuce leaves

Cut cucumbers in half lengthwise; scoop out seeds. Cut in one-fourth-inch-thick slices. Halve tomatoes, discard seeds and juice, and cut meat into three-fourths-inch pieces. Cut carrots into julienne strips (food processor may be used). Stir onion into cream cheese. Blend in sour cream, mayonnaise, and lemon juice. Fold in three tablespoons of the caviar and combine with vegetables. Chill. Serve in lettuce-lined bowl garnished with remaining caviar. Makes six servings.

CAVIAR-STUFFED AVOCADOS

3   ounces cream cheese, softened
¼   cup mayonnaise or salad dressing
½   cup minced celery
2   teaspoons lemon juice

few drops Tabasco
2   ripe avocados
4   tablespoons caviar
crisp salad greens

Into cream cheese, blend mayonnaise, celery, lemon juice, and Tabasco. Halve avocados lengthwise. Remove pits; peel. Brush with additional lemon juice. Set aside one tablespoon caviar. Fold remainder into cheese mixture. Use to fill hollows of avocados. Arrange on greens. Garnish with reserved caviar. Makes four servings.

HELP-YOURSELF SALAD WITH CAVIAR MAYONNAISE

2   zucchinis, peeled and cut in half-inch strips
2   carrots, cut in sticks
10 ribs of celery, cut in 2-inch pieces
20 cherry tomatoes, cut in half

1   cup mayonnaise
1   tablespoon caviar
1   teaspoon prepared mustard
1   teaspoon minced onion

When vegetables are pared, arrange on platter and chill. Combine remaining ingredients. Cover and chill until serving time. Guests may choose a relish and help themselves to dip. Enough for six.

Note: This dressing is also delicious with cold seafood or chilled cooked vegetables.

CAVIAR DRESSING FOR CHEF'S SALAD

½   cup mayonnaise
⅓   cup corn oil
¼   cup chili sauce
2   tablespoons wine vinegar

2   teaspoons lemon juice
3   tablespoons caviar
1   tablespoon parsley flakes
dash of pepper

Combine mayonnaise with next four ingredients. Fold in remaining ingredients. Cover and keep cold. At serving time, combine with foods for salad (see below). Makes about 1¼ cups, enough for six servings.

Chef's Salad. A good blend is 6 torn salad greens,

2 cups julienne ham, 2 cups julienne cheese, 1½ cups julienne chicken, and four hard-cooked eggs, quartered.

Baked Potatoes with Caviar

4   baking potatoes
¾   cup sour cream
2   tablespoons caviar

Prick skin of potatoes. If desired, rub with butter or margarine. Bake at 450°F. (hot oven) one hour or until fork tender. Cut an X in each potato; squeeze gently. Top with a dollop of sour cream and a heaping teaspoonful of caviar.

Gourmet Baked Potatoes. After baking, cut off thin horizontal slice from top. Fluff up potatoes with fork, then mash in one tablespoon butter or margarine, a squeeze of lemon juice, and a sprinkling of chopped chives. Top with sour cream and caviar as above.

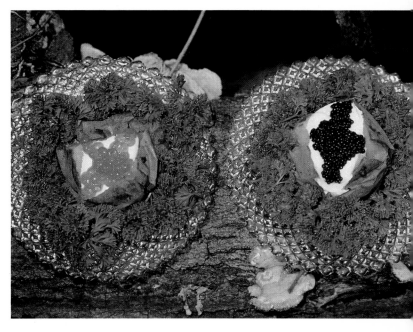

Baked potatoes with caviar. *Photo: Marlies Jung.*

ENTREES

Tomato Aspic with Caviar

1	cup hot water	2	envelopes unflavored gelatin
2½	cups tomato juice	½	cup cold water
⅓	cup chopped onion	¼	cup lemon juice
2	tablespoons sugar		sour cream
1	teaspoon salt	3	tablespoons caviar
1	bay leaf		

Place first six ingredients in saucepan; simmer ten minutes. Sprinkle gelatin over cold water in a medium-sized bowl. Strain tomato mixture into it, discarding onion and bay leaf. Stir until dissolved. Stir in lemon juice. (If desired, mixture may be poured into six-cup mold rinsed with cold water.) Chill three hours or until set. Serve topped with sour cream and caviar. Mixture may be spooned into sherbet or cocktail glasses before topping. Makes six to eight servings.

Spaghetti with caviar sauce. *Photo: Marlies Jung.*

SPAGHETTI WITH CAVIAR SAUCE

½ pound spaghetti
1 cup sour cream
½ cup heavy cream
3 tablespoons lemon juice

¼ cup butter
3 to 4 tablespoons caviar
    Parmesan cheese

Cook spaghetti according to label directions. Drain. Place on large heated platter. Meanwhile, in double-boiler top, combine sour cream, heavy cream, lemon juice, and butter. Cook over gently simmering water, stirring often, until hot. Fold in caviar. Pour over spaghetti. Sprinkle with cheese. Makes four servings.

CAVIAR CREPES

12 warm crepes
1 pint sour cream

1 cup caviar
½ cup finely chopped scallions

Spread sour cream down middle of each crepe. Sprinkle with caviar and scallions. Roll seam-side down. Top with more sour cream, caviar, and scallion. Makes twelve.

These photos illustrate how to make crepes and caviar. *Photos: Marlies Jung.*

Crepes: With rotary beater, beat 2 eggs, 2 tablespoons melted butter, and 1 cup milk. Add ¾ cup flour and ½ teaspoon salt. Beat until smooth. Cover. Chill one hour. To make crepe, melt a scant teaspoon butter in a seven-inch pan. Pour in about three tablespoons batter, swirl around bottom of pan. Cook over medium heat until sides begin to brown. With spatula, turn crepe and brown other side. Stack, separating with foil; keep warm until all are prepared. Makes twelve.

(You may also use a packaged mix to make the crepes.)

Omelettes with caviar.
Photo: Marlies Jung.

CAVIAR OMELET

3   eggs
¼   teaspoon salt
    dash pepper
1   tablespoon water
2   tablespoons butter or margarine

2   tablespoons sour cream
2   tablespoons caviar
    Additional sour cream and caviar
    for garnish

Beat together eggs, salt, pepper, and water. Heat butter in nine-inch skillet. When it sizzles, pour in eggs. Cook over medium heat, lifting cooked portion at edge with spatula to allow uncooked egg to flow underneath. When egg is nearly dry on top, spoon sour cream and caviar across one-third of omelet. Loosen edge with spatula, fold in thirds, and slide onto plate. Garnish with more sour cream and caviar. Serves one generously.

CAVIAR QUICHE

1   8-inch frozen pie shell
2   tablespoons butter or margarine
1   small onion, finely chopped
½   cup diced Swiss cheese
1   cup light cream
½   teaspoon salt

¼   teaspoon nutmeg
    dash pepper
2   eggs, lightly beaten
⅓   cup sour cream
2 to 3 tablespoons caviar

Place rack in center of oven and preheat to 400°F. Thaw shell twenty minutes. Flute edge to make high rim. In hot butter, cook onion until transparent. Place in pie shell with cheese. Combine eggs, cream, salt, nutmeg, and pepper. Pour over cheese. Bake pie on cookie sheet about forty minutes or until knife inserted in center comes out clean; cool on rack ten minutes. Gently spread with sour cream. Sprinkle with caviar. Cut into wedges. Makes four servings.

Caviar-stuffed Celery

1 bunch celery
8 ounces cream cheese, softened
2 tablespoons milk
1 tablespoon chopped chives

2 tablespoons chopped parsley
2 tablespoons caviar
additional caviar for garnish

Trim and wash celery stalks. Cut to make sixteen 2½-inch pieces. Mix cheese with milk until smooth. Stir in chives, parsley, and caviar. Spoon onto celery pieces. Cover. Chill. Just before serving, garnish with additional caviar. Makes sixteen pieces.

BUFFET DISHES

EGG-AND-CAVIAR SPREAD

8	hard-boiled eggs, chopped
¼	cup softened butter
2	teaspoons prepared mustard
½	cup caviar
3	tablespoons lemon juice
1½	tablespoons Worcestershire
4	tablespoons mayonnaise for garnish
	rye bread slices

Combine eggs, butter, mustard, and two-thirds (about five tablespoons) of the caviar with lemon juice and Worcestershire, blending well. Spoon into serving dish; cover and keep cold at least one hour. Just before serving, spread mayonnaise over top. Garnish with remaining caviar. Provide servers, so guests may spread on rye slices. Serves eight.

CAVIAR CROUTES

14	slices regular white bread
	softened butter or margarine
3	ounces cream cheese and chives, softened
3	tablespoons caviar
2	teaspoons lemon juice
14	pimiento strips

With two-inch biscuit butter, cut out two rounds from each bread slice. Spread half the slices with soft butter. With one-inch cutter, cut out center of remaining rounds. Place one rim on each whole round and spread with butter. Place on cookie sheet; bake at 400°F (hot oven) about ten minutes until browned. Cool. Divide cheese into centers. Combine caviar and lemon juice and spoon over cheese. Garnish with pimiento. Makes fourteen.

CAVIAR CUCUMBER ROUNDS

3	ounces cream cheese, softened
22	one-third-inch slices pared cucumber (from two small cucumbers)
3	tablespoons caviar
	lemon juice
22	small cocktail onions

Blend cream cheese and milk. Spread on cucumber slices. Spoon a little caviar in center of each. Sprinkle with lemon juice. Drain onions on paper towel and place one on each round, in center of caviar. Makes twenty-two.

Caviar-stuffed Mushrooms

¾ cup salad oil
¼ cup cider vinegar
1 garlic clove, coarsely chopped
 dash freshly ground black pepper
30 to 36 medium-size mushrooms (about 1 pound)
8 ounces cream cheese, softened
¼ cup mayonnaise
3 tablespoons minced onion
½ cup caviar

In shallow bowl, combine oil, vinegar, garlic, and pepper. Wash and remove stems from mushrooms. Coat caps with dressing; set aside, hollow side up. Combine cheese with mayonnaise and onion. Fill mushrooms with cheese; top each with rounded ¼ teaspoon caviar. Makes thirty to thirty-six stuffed mushrooms.

Caviar-stuffed Artichokes

12 ounces artichoke hearts in oil, drained
⅓ cup sour cream
2 teaspoons minced pimiento
½ teaspoon lemon juice
4 tablespoons caviar
20 to 24 Melba toast rounds
 Parsley sprigs for garnish

Pat artichoke hearts dry; set hollow side up. Combine sour cream, pimiento, lemon juice, and two tablespoons of the caviar. Fill artichoke hearts. Chill. Top with remaining caviar. Place each on a toast round and garnish with parsley. Makes twenty to twenty-four.

Confetti Dip

5 tablespoons milk
8 ounces cream cheese, softened
1 tablespoon chives

Caviar pie. *Photo: Marlies Jung.*

2 tablespoons chopped parsley
2 tablespoons caviar

Blend milk with cream cheese until mixture is easy to dip. Gently stir in remaining ingredients. Garnish with additional caviar if desired. Serve with raw vegetable relishes (below) or unsalted crackers. Makes 1¼ cups dip.

Raw Vegetable Relishes
1 bunch celery
1 cucumber
¼ pound very young green beans
4 carrots
½ head cauliflower
1 bunch radishes

Trim celery and cut into three-inch lengths. Peel cucumber and cut in half crosswise, then into half-inch-thick strips. Remove ends from beans. Peel carrots and cut into half-inch-thick strips. Cut cauliflower into florets. Pare radishes. Place vegetables in ice water at least one hour. Drain and serve with caviar dip. Serves 10.

Surprise Dip

1 cup sour cream
1 teaspoon lemon juice
4 tablespoons caviar

Combine all ingredients. Cover and chill. Serve with unsalted crackers or raw vegetable relishes. Makes about 1 cup dip.
(Yogurt lovers may substitute 1 cup plain whole-milk yogurt.)

HORS D'OEUVRES AND DIPS

Classic Caviar Serving

2 hard-boiled eggs, chopped fine
1 medium-size onion, minced
6 to 8 ounces sour cream or yogurt
       sweet butter or margarine

thin-sliced brown bread
white toast triangles
unsalted crackers
seeded lemon wedges
4 ounces caviar

Chill caviar and present in original container or glass cup nestled in a bowl of cracked ice. Surround with individual dishes of the egg, sour cream, butter, onion, and lemon wedges. Serve with the breads and crackers.

CAVIAR "PIE"

6 hard-boiled eggs, chopped
3 tablespoons mayonnaise
1 large sweet onion, finely chopped (1½ cups)
8 ounces cream cheese, softened

⅔ cup sour cream
7 tablespoons caviar
   lemon wedges and parsley sprigs for garnish

Grease bottom and side of eight-inch springform pan. In a bowl, combine eggs and mayonnaise until well blended. Spread in bottom of pan to make an even layer. Sprinkle with onion. Combine cream cheese and sour cream; beat until smooth. By the spoonful, drop onto onion. With a wet table knife, spread gently to smooth. Cover. Chill three hours or overnight. At party time, top with a layer of caviar, distributing it to the edges of the pan. Run knife around sides of pan, loosen, and lift off sides. Arrange lemon wedges in open pinwheel. Fill center with parsley sprigs. Serve with small pieces of pumpernickel bread. Makes ten to twelve servings.

ZHIVAGO'S DRESSING

1 cup mayonnaise
1 tablespoon well-drained horseradish
1 teaspoon lemon juice
2 tablespoons caviar

Combine mayonnaise, horseradish, and lemon juice. Gently stir in caviar. Cover and keep cold until ready to use. Delicious with cold vegetable salads, with cooked shrimp, or as a spread for unsalted crackers. Makes about 1 cup.

Elisabeth Stein cuts the caviar pie. *Photo: Marlies Jung.*

Here is a menu from a caviar-tasting party I recently conducted for the Wine and Food Society, Inc., of New York. It was held in the Belvedere Suite of the Rainbow Room.

Fresh Keta and Pasteurized Salmon Roe
Pasteurized Iranian and Russian Sevruga
Fresh Pressed Caviar Iranian
Fresh Sevruga Malossol Caviar Iranian
Fresh Osetra Malossol Caviar Iranian
Canadian and Russian Smoked Sturgeon
Fresh Beluga Malossol Caviar
Russian and Iranian

Perrier-Jouet Fleur de France, 1973
Stolichnaya Vodka

This was the menu for a caviar tasting held for the Arizona Chapter of Confrérie de la Chaîne des Rôtisseurs. It was held at the University Club of Phoenix.

Fresh Keta and Pasteurized Salmon Roe
Pasteurized Iranian and Russian Sevruga
(Served with Stolichnaya Vodka)
Canadian and Russian Sturgeon
Fresh Sevruga Malossol Iranian
Fresh Osetra Malossol
(Served with Taitinger Brut la Française)
Canadian and Scotch Smoked Salmon
Fresh Russian and Iranian Beluga Malosol

Salad

Cheese
(Served with Château Tetra Daugay, 1966)

SHRIMP WRAPPED IN CABBAGE LEAVES WITH CAVIAR BEURRE BLANC

Les Feuilles de Chou Farcies de Crevettes au
Beurre de Beluga

2 tablespoons oil
1 pound, 2 ounces very large shrimp in the
   shell (16 jumbo shrimp)
8 large outside loose leaves of cabbage (to get
   enough attractive, dark green leaves you will
   probably need 2 cabbages)
   salt and freshly ground black pepper
1 tablespoon plus 2 teaspoons unsalted
   butter, at room temperature
   Caviar Beurre Blanc (recipe follows)
2 teaspoons finely diced pimiento

Put the oil in a large sauté or frying pan placed
over high heat. Cook the shrimp in their shells,
turning them frequently until they just begin to
look opaque. (You want them slightly under-

cooked so that they will be perfectly cooked after reheating.) Remove each shrimp as it is cooked. Let the shrimp cool; then shell them and devein them.

Bring 2 quarts of water to a boil with 1 tablespoon salt. Have a bowl of ice water ready beside the stove. Boil 4 cabbage leaves at a time until tender but not soft, about 8 minutes. With a slotted spoon remove them to the ice water. When all the leaves are cooked and cooled, drain them and blot dry with paper towels. Cut out any tough core parts.

Arrange all the leaves on a board, outer sides down. Season lightly with salt and pepper. Divide the shrimp into 8 equal portions. Place a portion in the middle of a leaf. Fold in the bottom, then the sides and top to make a neat packet. Repeat with the remaining leaves and shrimp. Butter an 8-inch baking dish with 1 teaspoon butter. Place the packets folded sides down in the dish. Dot them with the remaining butter. (The packets can be prepared in advance to this point, covered airtight, and refrigerated. Let them come to room temperature before baking.)

Preheat the oven to 475° F. Cover the baking dish lightly with foil. Bake for 8 minutes, until thoroughly heated. Arrange on a serving platter or place 2 packets on each individual serving plate. Spoon 1 tablespoon of the Caviar Beurre Blanc over each packet. Garnish with the pimiento.

Makes 8 servings.

Caviar Beurre Blanc

1   ounce shallots (1 large or 2 medium), peeled
3   tablespoons white wine vinegar
2   tablespoons fish stock or clam broth
2   sticks (8 ounces) unsalted butter, chilled and cut into 15 pieces
1   tablespoon black caviar
    pinch cayenne pepper
    salt and freshly ground black pepper

To mince the shallot, put the metal blade in a

food processor, turn it on, and drop the shallot through the feed tube.

Put the minced shallot, vinegar, and fish stock or clam broth in a 1-quart saucepan. Cook over moderately high heat until the liquid has reduced by half. Strain out the shallots, return the liquid to the pan, and reduce to 1 tablespoon. Still over moderately high heat, add 3 butter pieces at a time and whisk continuously until the butter is absorbed before adding more butter. When all the butter has melted, add the caviar and cayenne, and salt and pepper to taste. Set the sauce aside on a warm stove or in a pan of warm water. If you must reheat it, do so over low heat, whisking constantly.

Reprinted by permission of *The Pleasures of Cooking* (Cuisinart Cooking Club, Inc.)

This license plate is on the car of Arnold Hansen-Sturm,
president of Hansen Caviar.

Jerry Stein's license plate. *Photo: Marlies Jung.*